From Patagonia To Australia

Also by Brenda Eldridge and published by Ginninderra Press

Poetry

The Silver Cord
It's All Good
A Personal View
Facing Cancer
From My Garden
Best Heard & Seen
Scarves
Tangled Roots: new & selected poems
Elemental (Pocket Poets)

Non-fiction

Down by the River
Tales From My Patagonia
It's Still Out There
There's a Rainbow Serpent In My Garden
Eastwards

Edited by Brenda Eldridge and published by Ginninderra Press

Brave Enough To Be a Poet
The Heart of Port Adelaide
Collecting Writers

Brenda Eldridge

From Patagonia
To Australia

Collected Prose

From Patagonia To Australia: Collected Prose
ISBN 978 1 74027 898 0
Copyright © Brenda Eldridge 2015
Cover photo: Stephen Matthews

First published in this form 2015 by
GINNINDERRA PRESS
PO Box 3461 Port Adelaide 5015
www.ginninderrapress.com.au

Contents

Introduction	7
Tales From My Patagonia	9
Down by the River	57
It's Still Out There	89
There's a Rainbow Serpent in my Garden	133
Eastwards	165

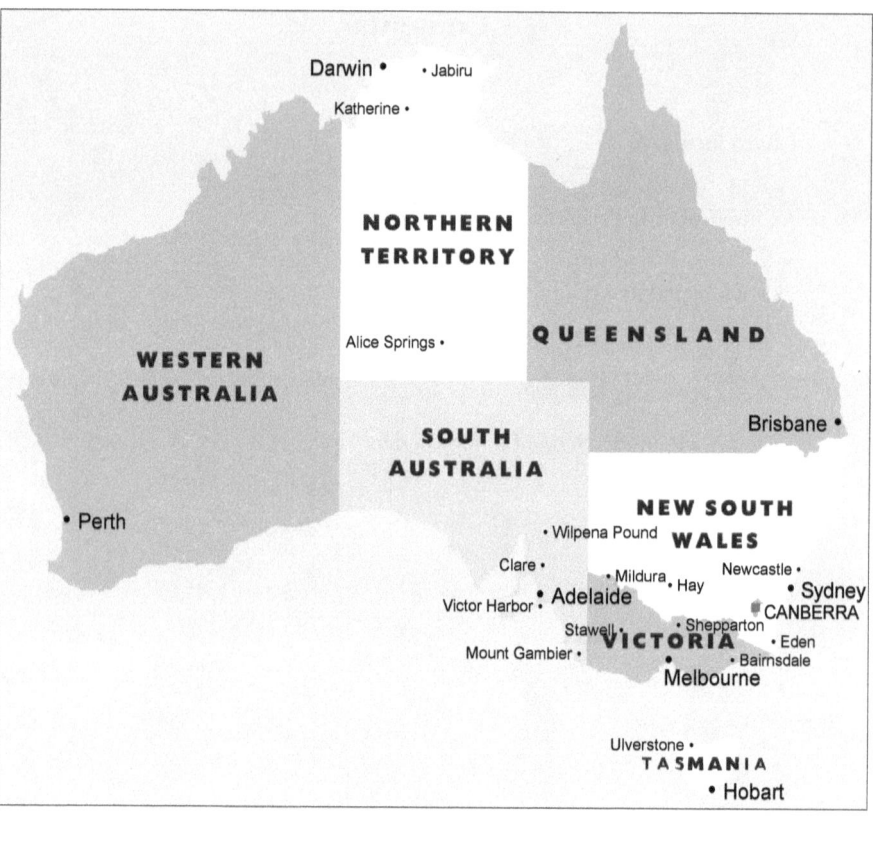

Introduction

The reasons people move from one side of the planet to the other are many and varied. For this young wife and mother, November 1970 heralded the start of a new life.

The change from north to southern hemisphere, the familiar routine of seasons disrupted, the different stars in the heavens, different customs and traditions, different climate – all of these things have been written about by migrants countless times. Many are tales of heartache and privation and I could have written an account containing all of those things.

Instead, when the time was right, I found myself writing about the wonders I had discovered in this extraordinary land called Australia – the place I have called home for all these years.

There are many things that connect us to places that have nothing to do with buying a plot of land and building a house on it. As a child growing up in the country, it was what I felt when I played in the beech woods and cherry orchards, or walked along narrow lanes flanked by high hazel and holly hedges, gathering wild flowers. I knew no angst. Growing up in a very old farmhouse with a resident ghost of a Roman soldier, feeling the presence of something or someone unseen was natural. I could not have identified it then, but it was a spiritual connection I was feeling with the past and the present.

Everything felt so new here in Australia. An unfair assessment perhaps, but none of the buildings gave me the sense of history I had grown up with. Yet when I started to explore and really look at how the land itself is formed, grew familiar with the vast skies, the changing seasons, the unusual animal and plant life, buried one of my sons in the red earth, and had two part-Aboriginal grandsons, I felt a spiritual connection here too.

The stories collected here from *Tales From My Patagonia*, *Down by the River*, *It's Still Out There*, *There's a Rainbow Serpent in My Garden* and *Eastwards* are like a running journal of discovery. There will be others, because my discoveries are not finished by any means and I always have to write things down to make them real. But with each trip out into what I now lovingly call my extended garden, I am free of angst and, while in some respects no longer the innocent child, I learn more and more why I have always felt so at home here.

Tales From My Patagonia

Prologue

While going through a difficult and frustrating period in my life, I was heard to mutter, 'I'm leaving home and I'm going to Patagonia.'
    One person said, 'Where's Patagonia?'
    A second said, 'Why Patagonia?'
    That set me thinking.
    Casually asking around, I found a lot of people weren't quite sure where Patagonia is and seemed genuinely surprised when I said, 'Bottom of South America, on the right hand side of Chile.' (Right and left, top and bottom being easier to grasp than north, south, east and west.}
    As to why Patagonia: simply because few people do know where it is and I felt it would be a good place to go to find some solitude.
    Aware of the inevitability of reality, I will confess here at the beginning that I have never been to the geographical location of Patagonia. My tales are a collection of observations of living in South Australia for many years.
    Why did I write them? Chapter one tells how I overcame my fears and made myself cross a foot suspension bridge. After that, I felt I could overcome anything. I began looking at my adopted corner of the world through different eyes. I have been blessed with a grasshopper mind. My memories are, therefore, linked by themes and have a random, rolling quality, often coming full circle.
    I hope, through these tales, others will find their own Patagonia.

One

I sat at the bus stop for over half an hour and lost count of the buses that pulled in. None of them was the correct number to take me home. An idea sprang from hidden depths and a quiet little voice whispered, 'You could walk there by the time the right bus comes along.'

On such simple words are great adventures embarked upon. Prudence took my footsteps to a delicatessen to purchase a bottle of water. I had a small packet of potato crisps and an almond and apricot cookie in my bag. What more could I need? So with one last hesitant pause, I set forth the quickest way I knew from busy streets and crowded shopping malls to the relative quiet of the riverbank.

The river had been excavated to form a lake in the city centre. Big trees were left to admire their own reflections, which were more than worthy of praise. Leaves shivered with every passing breeze and, depending on which way that breeze was blowing, they shimmered darkest green or the silver-white sheltered and hidden on their underside.

People from all walks of life strolled along the pathways.

Dedicated young parents took their children for the mandatory walk in the park to feed the ducks. Ducks are always so very obliging and come with insatiable appetites quite happy to accept the offerings. I don't think they were too fussed whether the bread was homemade and rich in natural fibre or commercially produced with the required number of slices per loaf.

Nurses in their precise uniforms meandered, glad of an opportunity to unwind from a heavy, and too often distressing, workload at the nearby hospital.

Businessmen in suits, regardless of the weather, strolled tensely, rapidly devouring their meat pies, shedding jackets as a concession to the warmth, carrying them with studied casualness over one shoulder but leaving ties still carefully knotted. You never knew if you would see the boss or that future prospective client out taking the air, and it wouldn't do to appear as if off duty during office hours.

Women strode along, hiding their femininity underneath severely tailored suits, carefully eating healthy salad sandwiches or a meagre piece of fruit, planning their next conquest whether in the commercial world or of a new lover. A passing vision crossed my mind of a forgotten time when ladies walked gracefully like swaying flowers in a garden, bedecked in the finest materials accentuating hidden, curvaceous delights.

Cyclists and joggers dashed past, faces crimson, sweat pouring into the required uniform of old T-shirt. Did they see themselves as the next Olympic champions or were they trying to find a shape that would fit into the fantasies of those tailored ladies?

Then there were the students, of course, the lake and parklands being the back garden of the university. Theirs a statement of studied defiance, earnest young minds questing for knowledge – theorising about the world which no doubt they will change one day, possibly for the better.

There was even a scattering of romantic lovers, quietly talking as they lusted for each other, wishing the area were free of people so they could lie on the inviting grass and get totally lost.

Following a spontaneous thought, I walked across the arched university footbridge rather than cross the road bridge to get to the other side of the lake. I imagined myself a terribly serious contemplative student, full of my own self-importance. One day my brilliance was going to amaze the world. When I am ninety-seven, I will cycle along the High Street of Oxford, waving my philosophy degree in my hand, the oldest graduate from the university. Ah well, who knows?

I watched mum and dad black swan. Their three babies of a few weeks ago had grown from balls of fluff into fine youths, as yet lacking their parents' grace.

I smiled at the man sitting on the grass with a fishing rod who was being cleverly harassed by a pelican. I couldn't see what the pelican had in mind to relieve him of, but it certainly was determined. I recalled a book I read once, long ago, something to do with people accepting without question a man standing on a bridge, or sitting beside a river with a stick and a piece of string, but suspecting ill-intent if the same man were empty-handed. I wondered if my man was mentally fishing without a rod.

I walked over carefully manicured lawns and past well tended rose gardens to the wilds at the back of the zoological gardens. I heard monkeys screeching, and a lion roar, and wished I could go in and release them all. Seriously, though, where would they be left in peace to eat their lunch? Nowhere! It was a sobering thought.

Gradually I was leaving the city behind me. Tall, graceful gum trees, casting luxurious shadows, lined the passage of the river. It travelled dark green and as if unmoving till a cluster of rocks broke the surface and caused it to form into miniature rapids. The sun sparkled off the white swirling wavelets and made them light-hearted messengers of joy, a stark contrast to the almost sinister mainstream.

I paused in the midday heat at a weir. Wooden seats were set decorously and symmetrically in a semicircle. As I ate my lunch of salty crisps and lukewarm water, I watched an egret. He was poised on a rock, unmoving as a grey-clad novice of the church, scanning the still pool just above the weir, waiting to stab passing lunch. His efforts were rewarded as his head bobbed down and up. A flash of silver was held captive in his menacing beak. A water rat held me entranced for ages, so smoothly did his sleek body cut a perfect V through the brown muddy water. Was he too in search of lunch hiding amid the reeds?

I glanced upriver and there, in the near distance, the Ultimate Challenge. The foot suspension bridge! I watched in awe as a young girl strode with purposeful steps over the span. She was probably about twenty years old, with a small compact body that she obviously took care of with proper diet and exercise. Her blonde hair was scraped up into a ponytail and bounced as she strode along. She wasn't deterred for a moment by the rocking motion or the awful creaking of the bridge.

I jokingly said, 'You're very brave.'

She grinned and replied, 'You can do it,' and gaily walked on, calling back, 'Have a good day.'

I abstractedly returned her greeting.

I stood at the beginning of the bridge, feet still firmly on the ground. What a dreadful height the bridge reached! Well, it was probably forty feet at its highest. How deadly the waters below! Any water is deadly if you don't swim and it certainly wasn't deep enough to perform an elegant swan dive into without coming to a sticky end, even if I knew how. Supposing the bridge swayed and I was tipped over the side? I clutched the rope handrail and stepped onto the green-painted slatted surface. My heart stopped and so did my feet. I admonished myself severely and pushed my feet forward in small shuffling steps. In my mind I talked to a friend. He is always in the middle of me and makes me brave. I feebly defended my cowardice and gave in to his laughing blue eyes and inched my way across, my stomach lurching in keeping with the gentle movement of the bridge.

My imagination took off. Far, far below me a raging river galloped in tumbling waves over craggy rocks, spray and mist flying high, filled with rainbows. The face of the mountainside ahead was sheer and unflinching rock, no mercy there. High above, on the other side, my minuscule bridge climbed to a safe landing. Would I have to pull myself up the last thousands of feet to reach it? That wretched little voice inside started up again. 'Don't look down and don't stop. If your feet stop moving, I can't guarantee we can start them up again, and how long do you think you can stand, frozen on a foot suspension bridge a million feet from the Earth's surface?'

What felt like hours later, my feet stepped onto the hard red earth on the other side of the river. A large native lilac tree swayed gently and its beautifully fragrant blossoms were alive with the humming of bees.

I turned around, half filled with a glowing sense of achievement – half filled with dread. After all, I still had to get back across the bridge. I grasped the handrail again, took a very deep breath and shuffled my way, even slower, back. Such was my relief to get across safely, I literally began looking about me through different eyes. For that brief time, I had been the likes of Indiana Jones in South America, in search of a place hardly anyone knew of. It might just as well have been Patagonia.

I continued my walk along the river path, still in my Patagonia. I was glad of my long-sleeved shirt, as the sun had quite a sting to it. Several mynah birds swooped persistently, their warning calls far-reaching. I wondered what all the noise was about, till I looked down among the bark beside the path and saw a long-tailed lizard slowly making his way up the bank. He blended in perfectly with his surroundings and only the soft rustling of his moving body gave his presence away – and those garrulous mynah birds. So much for his quiet afternoon constitutional!

I passed a bush I had not knowingly seen before. At first I thought it was a strawberry bush then reminded myself that was silly; after all, strawberries grow close to the ground and this bush towered up several feet over my head, which made it all of eight or nine feet tall. So what was the pretty and lush red fruit so reminiscent of a strawberry?

I sat on a solitary bench and ate half of my almond and apricot cookie. A young couple earnestly strode past. Hikers always make me feel slow and aimless.

The young Adonis announced to the world in a carelessly arrogant tone, 'Would you like a mulberry, dear? The best are at the top.'

His partner softly declined and they ploughed on debating what wonder was to be encountered around the bend.

I hoped it was a nice surprise for them – my interest in caravan parks was very limited, but at least I knew what a mulberry bush looked like now. I'm sure there was a nursery rhyme – 'Here we go round the mulberry bush so early in the morning' – in my distant childhood.

I wandered along and came across a particularly beautiful area of lush, bright grass and grand gums spread before me. I could hear exotic parrots calling to each other. I searched in vain for a glimpse of those bright scarlet, orange, yellow, purple and green bodies. However, looking up among the branches, I espied man-made nesting boxes, each carefully numbered and fastened to a branch by wide webbing for minimum damage. I chuckled at the vision of a postman delivering mail. Fleetingly I was back in my childhood among the storybooks about Blackberry Farm and Joe Robin the postman. I was a long way from England but not so far from the child within, apparently.

Every country, it seems, has its old, toothless men. This one scrambled down a steep bank and started talking in an agitated tone. He had ancient brown trousers and a white shirt with rolled-up sleeves. He reminded me just a little of my dad when he laboured in the garden on summer evenings tending vegetables for his growing and ever-hungry family. This man's five o'clock shadow beard said it was more like ten o'clock and I couldn't begin to imagine what he needed a white plastic supermarket bag for. Fortunately for us both perhaps, I had no knowledge of the language he was using, but it didn't include *buenas dias* so I figured it was eastern European. Or maybe it was no-teeth English.

I kept walking and he turned away and talked to a brood of very tiny baby ducklings on what looked like their first outing on the river. They were riding some of those miniature rapids I mentioned earlier. I thought they were a trifle small for duck à l'orange, but then who knew what his cultural background had taught him? Christopher Columbus had a lot to answer for!

My gaze seemed to rove with a will of its own and my mind registered that there were fascinating little beetles here in my Patagonia. So many scuttling from right to left across the path, black at first glance. However, when the sun lighted on their backs, they were brilliant metallic green. Almost too good to be real, but I saw so many I stopped rejecting their impossible beauty and accepted it joyfully. Dragonflies too, big and small, skittered and hovered over the river, darted over to check me out then off again. Some were soft tortoiseshell-brown, others looked as if they had gone too close to the sky and dipped the tips of their bodies in the blueness.

My back was beginning to ache and that incessant little voice started a litany of 'Are we nearly there? I'm tired. I need a carry.'

'Well, be quiet, do. I don't know if we're nearly there.'

Suburbia kept slurping down to the pathway like some insidious, unstoppable ooze. The houses looked too precise to be the warm, friendly homes of children with barking dogs overflowing onto the lawns. The gardens all immaculately kept, even the flowers nodded at the required angle in the passing breeze. There was nothing too ostentatious – just an appalling effort at gentility that looked unnatural and clinical. Even audacious weeds dared not show their faces between the pavers and definitely no wisps of grass peeped out of the eaves where a sparrow might have built its nest.

My heart cheered up distinctly when I came across a totally different style of house, all big, clean-cut windows and very modern. Best of all, it was painted golden yellow all over except the royal blue window frames. How their neighbours must have bridled, gasped and flustered when that little lot was created.

At some stage, I looked over my shoulder and, without my realising it had happened, the bank had risen high above the river and cliffs of red and ochre dwarfed all the bushes and trees in the riverbed. Suddenly it didn't matter how long it took to get home; I was free and it was a glorious day.

Eventually, to the left, I came to a flight of steps crawling up the hillside. My home nestled in the garden of a tumbling riot of pink, white, yellow, orange and red flowers. There was nothing at all formal about this. The windows winked in welcome. My wooden rocking chair sat waiting on the balcony. It was good to be home. I plodded up the steps and counted seventy-one, or was it seventy-three? By the time I climbed to the top, I was looking down on the roof. Tiredly I walked down the steep drive, and let myself into another world of calm and peace. After a quick shower to get rid of the dust, I lay on my bed. The silence seeped into my weary being and I teetered on the brink between sleeping and waking.

Every window of the house looked out over green foliage, be it grass, bushes or ivy-covered garden walls. Enormous gum trees grew all around and I was high up enough to look down on the winding river. Well, it was only a little creek linking a series of large, deep ponds. The reeds hid the water but they were so bright it was easy to trace the meandering path. I could not see any of my neighbours' houses either side or across the river, only a patch of roof or chimney here and there. In the near distance, the hills rose in majestic glory. They were tree-covered and did a marvellous impersonation of a gigantic sleeping dragon.

I noticed it had taken four hours of solid plodding to get home!

After an hour's rest, I took my pushbike from the study – well, why not, indeed: doesn't everyone keep a pushbike in the study? Locking up the house, I sailed off back to the river path. The air was warm and filled with the fragrance of flowers and blossoms. The sun was starting to sink lower in the western sky and when the pathway dipped into shadows the air was quite cool.

Egrets, herons and waterfowl roved peacefully on the grass. Those shiny beetles now were bustling back the other way across the path. Amazing toadstools, exhibiting the most stupendous colours of orange and brown and cream, and extraordinary shapes, clustered in hidden corners. Any old tree stump or lichen-covered bark had all kinds of unusual petticoats laced around them.

Other nature-lovers appeared, some industriously striding along – probably relatives of those I saw in the city at the beginning of my journey. There were older couples ambling contentedly with their equally elderly dogs. A vague notion developed: who was actually walking whom?

I passed an inventive father guiding a young child on her first bike with an amazing attachment to the back with which he could help her stay upright without training wheels. I'm not very mechanical, so the intricacies of this were lost on me but it certainly seemed to be working till she set up a plaintive wail that her legs were tired. I felt a kinship with this child, as my legs often had the same problem.

Everyone was cheerful and friendly with their greetings and blissfully enjoying the evening's serenity.

The next morning, the balcony pulled me with some magnetic force. I sat out there initially to eat my breakfast and share my toast with blackbirds and sparrows. I ended up with my mind drifting over the years of discovery…

Two

That morning, the wind had swept off the hills bringing rain, the simplest yet most precious of gifts. The honeyeaters up in the trees kept shaking themselves off like so many industrious matrons, shaking out their feather dusters. The gutter was dripping, perhaps telling me there were fallen leaves blocking the clear run of water. It was calm and restful as if some kindly presence was ironing out my wrinkles.

The earth smelled wonderful, having soaked up the raindrops. I had visions of all the tiniest little roots wriggling in excitement and anticipation when they began to take in the moisture like babies at a mother's breast. I wondered how long it took for that wetness to seep upward to every living portion of the plant, be it sky-blue lobelia, fiery nasturtium or giant gum tree. Imagine being so full they explode forth with new leaves and flowers like toes bursting out of old socks.

Equipped with bicycle pump and backpack containing an extra drink and a cheese-and-lettuce bread roll, a notepad and pen, I set off on the bike. Not for me Sunday-best clothing, going to church like the good parishioners I passed. I am sure St Francis of Assisi was pleased to have such a congregation. I met him, you know, a bit later on, out at Morialta Falls. We walked a while. We didn't say much because we could both see the same things, so words were superfluous.

The lady with the ice cream van had a spot in the car park at Morialta Falls. She made delicious hot doughnuts and reminded me, as I munched on mine, that I wasn't allowed to take my bike past that point. I chained it to a post with instructions to behave and the vendor looked after my helmet. I bought a bag of her tomatoes as a thank you.

St Francis and I began wandering very slowly along the pathway to the falls. The walls of the gorge tower up hundreds of feet – not like at the bridge to my Patagonia. This was truly awesome. Layers and layers of red rock, similar to the smaller cliffs of the riverbed, climbing so high I had to lean my head back as far as it would go to see the top. I felt so small and insignificant. The lower slopes were densely covered in nameless and many varied shades of green bush. Even the tallest gums were dwarfed. Shrubs and grasses had taken root in every conceivable crevice, covering the sides of these natural bastions. A far cry from the aubretia-covered rockery in the garden across the lane from where I grew up. This was a good lesson in humility.

My country upbringing was nudging me from far-off years. Yes, I did recognise that song as the wren. Not the shy, dull, brown bird of England. Here the male is the most brilliant blue imaginable, darting about with just a flash of colour and a long, pertly upright tail. I stood transfixed, leaning against the parapet of a bridge over the stream and watched him darting about, calling to his drab mate. I saw her long enough to notice she had the brightest black eyes I think I have ever seen on such a tiny bird. Their song had a piercing clarity that was almost unbearable to listen to. It reminded me a little of those gifted ladies who sing soprano, when you know the piece and you hold your breath as they build up to this fantastic pitch and hit the highest note with impeccable accuracy and, as the listener, you sigh with relief.

I climbed up some rocky steps to the Giant's Cave. It was easy to imagine someone seeking refuge here, lighting a fire to cook supper and sheltering from the night. I kept going upwards, turned, and there, clinging to the very top of the cave, a heaving mass of bees had swarmed. I'm not very brave about these creatures but I was spellbound by this frenzied gathering. A group of Asian people came up behind, chattering in a language unknown to me. I pointed the swarm out to an elderly woman in the party. The wonder on her face was beautiful to see. The younger ones were not so impressed. Perhaps she had seen enough horror in her life that she could appreciate the miracle before her.

My contemplation and appreciation of my surroundings was being constantly intruded upon by those wretchedly enthusiastic hikers. Do they only know how to stride to their destination? Don't they know that if you sit on the ground beneath a big tree, back leaning against a sun-warmed rock, you see the tiniest of finches hanging upside down, then suddenly zooming off to do a victory roll while catching lunch on the wing? Do they know that clusters of gum nuts look just like miniature church bells and chime in the wind?

I had intended sitting at the base of the falls and writing a poem but I was faced with the superfluousness of words. What can one say about water cascading over a rock face and plunging into a pool below? Better to go and see for yourself, really. St Francis and I strolled back to the car park.

My lady of the ice cream van watched as I fiddled with the mudguard of the bike to stop it rubbing on the tyre and surprised me when she called out, 'Go carefully.'

It was heart-warming. How many times have I said 'Take care' as my loved ones and even those not so well known have left me behind?

Three

Sparrows are the same the world over.

Another Sunday morning, after a cup of tea, I looked at the bike and heard that little voice say, 'Well, why not?' I now know it takes an hour and a half to cycle to the beach at Semaphore. Going home was definitely going to take longer as the last several kilometres were uphill. One doesn't notice such small details tootling about in cars. I wondered if I would run out of legs before I reached safe harbour.

I mentioned the sparrows because, on arriving at Semaphore, I sat at a sidewalk café. Having demolished a hot ham and cheese croissant and started on my second cup of coffee, I noticed that the flaky escapees from the croissant had been ardently picked up from between cracks in the pavement by several of these permanently busy and always homely little creatures. I wondered if sparrows have the same superstitions that we do about cracks in the pavement? Wasn't it Christopher Robin who had a thing about them? Perhaps I should consult the complete works of A.A. Milne on the bookshelf at home.

I had planned a swim to cool off when I arrived at the beach. Instead, I huddled under my jumper and decided it was extremely unlikely my simple, classic black bathers underneath would get wet – unless it rained, which looking at the sky seemed quite possible. Ah! What a coward.

I was under the distinct impression that the thriving metropolis of Semaphore hadn't woken up yet. It looked like just the locals popping into the continental cake shop for fresh bread and newspapers. I glanced in at the cake shop. I was bemused by so many different kinds of bread, all shades from white to darkest brown and countless variations in between. Soft or crisp crusts covered in poppy or sesame seeds. The aroma took me back to the days when the local baker delivered our bread on Tuesday, Thursday and Saturday nights. Just a plain oblong loaf; no such thing as sliced bread then. But that smell! They don't make bread like that any more.

The beach I found in my Patagonia was superb. Only a small cove held together by outstretched rocky promontories. I suppose sea walls would be a more accurate description, made up of enormous boulders placed as naturally as possible. Was it to guide boats upriver on one side and to the marina on the other? I could ask a nautically minded friend for clarification – well, I would if it were important.

The dunes were of sand so white that when the sun did eventually appear they dazzled my eyes. I remembered a story my mother used to tell long, long ago of how I cried at Brighton beach in the south of England because I didn't like the 'mud'. My memories are more of the sharp shingle we had to brave in bare feet to get to the freezing cold water of the English Channel.

The pale apricot wet sand was littered with all kinds of shells. Some were joined in the middle and lay like sleeping butterflies; the joins were so fragile, though, they often parted when I picked them up. I found cuttlefish everywhere – enough for a million caged birds. Maybe in my Patagonia the people are more compassionate and allow their beautiful feathered folk to fly free. I hoped so. I always want to let birds out when I see them in cages. I wondered what the fur balls were. Like small bundles of coconut fibre crowded together for warmth. Where was that nautically minded friend?

I settled on the soft dry sand and drifted off to another time and place in a book. The wind kept trying to turn the pages for me. I looked up now and again to watch a sailing ship, or should that be yacht, out on the water. Some moron with no appreciation for silence or respect for marine life was careering about somewhere on a jet ski. I hoped a passing whale would tip him over and his shark mate could eat him for lunch. We can but dream.

It was like a dream to see a dolphin offshore. Like the waterfall and the wren whistling, words were out of place. I felt humbled and honoured in its presence.

Time passed – they don't have watches in my Patagonia. The wind freshened – hey, the nautical stuff rubbed off; next I would be talking about sou'westers. No, that was Christopher Robin again in his galoshes. Anyway, it began to rain. Action! I hastily shoved glasses, book and clothes into a waterproof bag and headed for the water. Once in, I wondered why

I had not gone in earlier. The water wasn't the exquisite pale blues and greens like when the sun shone but it was so soft and warm, embracing my body as the wind and rain struck chill. The contrast was heavenly. I played as long as I could but inevitably the cold became too much.

I dried off quickly, the last thing I did do quickly, and cycled back to the café for some lunch. There were certainly more people about now but I struck another difficulty. The wind was stronger and not going the same way I was, which made pedalling hard work. Well, there really wasn't any other way to get home, so off I went. Thankfully the road turned a corner and the wind didn't, so it was easy. Except my legs were getting tired even on the flat bits and I'm sure someone had changed the saddle while I wasn't looking and replaced it with one cast in concrete or, at the very least, carved out of mahogany.

The first hill loomed ominously. With quaking heart, I kept going, then with trembling legs had to get off and walk. At least I could hang my shoulder bag and helmet on the handlebars. Head down, I plodded, imagining a friend, nautically minded or otherwise, appearing out of nowhere beside me in a car saying cheerfully, 'Hop in and I'll give you a ride home.' It didn't happen. That was the first hill. I scooted along a flattish stretch and the second hill was there. Not as steep, it's true, but where had my legs gone? Another walk. I was not impressed by the third one.

I know it was smooth sailing – oops, nautical again – smooth *cycling* from the top of that last hill to home but I didn't care a whole lot by then. I was cold, tired and feeling distinctly sick. This wasn't supposed to happen. I limped into the house some three hours after I had left the beach. I had a blissfully hot shower and crawled into bed not to emerge till twelve hours later.

So there you are. There are hills in my Patagonia. And wonderful oceans and sand dunes with skylarks and swallows…

Four

From my reading, I have placed the home of kite-flying squarely in Tibet. There, they make kites big enough to support a man. The idea is that the kite, with passenger, is launched off the side of a cliff and hopefully the upward air current will send everything soaring aloft. I haven't worked out how they manage to come back to earth again. Perhaps it is a once-in-a-lifetime escapade.

I wondered if this was the forerunner to hang-gliding. I must admit I like the idea of running along a grassy field and leaping off the edge of a cliff and flying. Imagine floating gracefully, whirling and twirling like an autumn leaf before landing softly as a feather on a conveniently placed grassy meadow below. The biggest problem, as I see it, is the actual landing. Having broken the same ankle twice, I am most reluctant to put undue stress on it. The first time I broke it was as a little girl. My mother would take my older brothers to school and then, with me sitting on the seat of her bicycle, she would stand up to pedal us home. This saved her a lot of time, only having to walk one way. However, this dreaming child was carried away swinging my legs and my ankle became entangled in the spokes of the wheel. The only thing I really remember was being upset because my shoe was stuck in the spokes after I had been extricated.

The second accident occurred over thirty years later. I discovered if you go to one of those adult playgrounds and throw caution to the wind by going down the biggest slippery dip, the one with the humpy-bumpy bits, straight after a downpour of rain, you go much too fast. I proved that in those conditions the sandpit at the bottom doesn't stretch anywhere near far enough and the grass might have looked soft but that was an illusion. I made a most undignified landing, finally ending up several metres from the bottom of the slide, with a chipped bone in my already damaged ankle. Having come back to earth with such an almighty thump, I now view landing from a very different perspective.

While on my many trips to the beach, I have often seen people flying kites on the unhindered expanses of sand. There was even a kite expo one day. There were kites of all sizes and colours: little ones that whizzed, buzzed and whined in tight circles like angry insects and larger more graceful ones. I was fascinated by one shaped like an enormous lime-green frog. It was anchored to the ground by pegs and as the wind gusted through it, it looked exactly as if we were on the bottom of a pond looking up at a frog swimming across the surface. Surprisingly there were no dragon kites but a wonderful assortment of dolphins, sharks, sea serpents and even a deep-sea diver.

The organisers were reputed to have the largest kite in the world to show off and on a calm day it needed to be weighed down by a large truck containing sand. Unfortunately the wind was too strong this day and they could not risk letting it fly. It conjured up lovely pictures, though. A kite floating across the neighbourhood with a truck sailing below it.

Apparently, kite-flying can be an expensive hobby if you are a real enthusiast. I fell in love with one built like a sailing ship. It was about two feet high and two feet long. All the sails were rainbow-coloured. My son managed to get it aloft for me. I never tried but, for a while, it sailed sedately across the lounge held aloft by strings.

I love to watch the men and women on their three-wheeler buggies racing along the sands being dragged, at great speed, by gigantic kites. From what I have seen, they are attached to the kites with harnesses. The kites are shaped much like the oblong parachutes that skydivers use. To have the brightest colours appears to be the order of the day.

On one particular day there were two of these buggies racing up and down. A third kite was billowing and bouncing on the sand, seemingly (to my ill-informed eyes) to be anchored by the hand pieces. One of the men decided to change kites but just as he settled into the buggy an extra strong gust of wind blew off the ocean and the whole thing tipped over. The driver was thrown clear of the buggy but the kite must have sensed freedom because it was away. The poor man was pulled unceremoniously along the sands. Fortune smiled on him and he was quickly able to stop and anchor the kite safely. Knowing how sharp the shells could be, I hurried over to see if he was hurt. He ruefully admitted he was panicking there for a moment or two, otherwise only his pride was damaged. Like me, he had envisioned himself sailing over the dunes and landing in a garden.

Before this incident, I had been thinking how much I would like to have a go as a passenger. I doubt that the kites would have moved the buggies with two people on board. Nice little dream, though.

As it happened, that same day there were three young men windsurfing backwards and forwards across the cove. Their sails made them look like big butterflies. They went so fast and I was transfixed, as suddenly one would do a complete somersault. Then they changed tactics and went racing out to sea, turned around and sped back to shore. My instinct was to open my arms to catch them. I received cheery waves and big smiles. I fancy they were showing off a little for my benefit and I was a delighted and appreciative audience. I could hear that dream voice hungering to have a go. Oh, what a nuisance having feet of clay.

Naturally with all that wind sport being on display, my thoughts inevitably turned to hot-air balloons. Now there was a fascinating mode of travel. There is a place in my Patagonia called the Barossa Valley, where an annual three-day event takes place. Balloonists come from all over the world to flaunt their magnificent treasures. There is something ethereal about dawn and dusk skies filled with gigantic silent balloons in fabulous colours and designs. I hadn't realised how many different shapes a hot-air balloon can be made into, even two-tiered ones. They appear to float so effortlessly, but I am sure the balloonist would correct the illusion of effortlessness. No doubt it takes great skill and effort to keep them afloat without bumping into trees, electricity cables and each other.

I was a little disappointed when I screwed up enough courage to go up as a passenger in a glider. I envisioned that I would have the sensation of soaring and sweeping through the air, with arms outstretched. Instead, the earth below gave the appearance of tipping and moving. I must add that the view was remarkable and the silence sublime, broken only by the whistling wind. I watched the sun set into a froth of cream and yellow clouds over the ocean from about two thousand feet. I was left speechless. It was another of those waterfall things, where you must go and do it for yourself. Somehow I didn't much care how we landed. I was mesmerised by that sunset.

I must confess to being secretly proud of myself for making that trip. I feel less inhibited about the feet of clay that have developed since.

Five

Many years ago I watched a documentary set in Africa. Monkeys and ostriches were weaving and falling about drunkenly after eating fruit from some enormous trees. I had no reason to doubt what I saw. However, there must have been some lingering disquiet. Not any longer!

At the bottom of my garden were several cumquat trees. Standing on my porch, I watched a couple of crows and some noisy parrots feasting on the ripened fruit. After a while, I noticed the crows kept falling out of the trees and fluttering not very gracefully onto the ground. With an outraged 'craark' they heaved and scrabbled back up into the tree only to repeat the process with studied care. It took a while for me to realise they were as drunk as the monkeys on fermenting fruit.

Pine trees, of course, grow all over the world, in varying shapes and many shades of green. Here in my Patagonia they are completely unorthodox. At different times I have seen them laden with clusters of large cones and, hanging upside down off the cones, emerald green parrots. They remind me a little of those ice creams where you stack scoops of different flavours one on top of the other. I have often wondered how you eat those ice creams without them toppling over. It is probably one of life's little mysteries that needs practical application to resolve.

Another pine tree looked like a giant Christmas tree. It was covered with countless white sulphur-crested cockatoos perched like candles waiting to be lit up. Imagine the uproar if you tried to do that!

One afternoon, the local bird life was in a terrible state, all sounding a continuous alarm. From the balcony I could see a boobook owl sitting in the pine tree. He sat so still he could have been carved of wood. He ignored the irate attacks of the little honeyeaters and wagtails. When he was good and ready, he flew off somewhere up the river and everyone's ruffled feathers were calmed. He came back some hours later and chaos broke out again. This distressing situation went on for three days before he finally left, and he hasn't yet returned.

By far the most unusual appendage to a pine tree was a swarm of bees looking and sounding like a very angry football. I wondered if 'up there, Cazaley' would have 'upped' there to get that ball. (For the blissfully uninitiated, Cazaley was an Australian rules footballer with an amazing capacity to leap high, climbing up the backs of fellow players to get the ball. Another of those 'you had to be there' things.)

There was one more tree that I loved, standing in my lounge. It was technically a couple of dead, twiggy branches, balanced in a large pot. The whole thing was covered in butterfly shells that jiggled and danced every time I opened or closed the French window curtains. For me to be contrary Mary properly, it needed to have silver bells and cockleshells. That was all very well, but did I really have to have the pretty maids all in a row?

Six

My Patagonia has staggering weather. It is difficult to try and explain day after day of over one-hundred-degree Fahrenheit temperatures. Even that is manageable if the nights are cool, but like most people I had this preconceived notion that the sun goes down, night falls, maybe the moon shines and a bunch of stars appear, but definitely, there is a drop in temperature. I'm sure the thermostat became stuck somewhere in times like those. Actually I am told the real explanation has something to do with the wind blowing off the deserts in the north-east rather than off the sea from the south-west. It is so simple when you know how.

Even the sparrows weren't too partial to that prolonged heat. Sometimes they came down to the porch and sat all fluffed up with beaks open panting for breath. Even if I put a dish of water out there, they didn't drink from it. With the river – um, correction, the series of ponds lying in the riverbed – so close, I thought they would have just popped down there for a quick pint.

I wonder why kookaburras laugh at night? They seemed to travel in pairs; well, in the summer anyway. One would start calling a certain way and the mate would call back. It sounded to me like he had been out on the town and come home having had one or two too many and she was giving him a good telling off. Probably it was nothing like that, but who knows – I bet David Attenborough does.

The searing heat has a startling effect on the gum trees. The bark on trunk and branches is a beautiful mixture of silvery grey and brown patches, smooth to the touch in most types of gum trees. Gradually the heat dries the bark out, causing it to crack and peel off a bit like dried old paintwork. The winds that never seem to stop for long, regardless of the heat, then proceed to strip great shards of bark from the trees and toss them to the ground. There they curl up lengthways and remind me of expensive cigars.

Meanwhile, the tree trunks and branches take on a totally different countenance. They become a moist, rich cream with lingering patches of silver. Their texture is so soft and damp to touch. In this state of transformation they look much like maps of treasure islands with curving coastlines and inland lakes. The heat has a much more deadly effect on the trees, creating what are locally called 'widow makers'. As a house settles at night and its timbers creak and grumble in the cooling air, so too do the trees. I had heard of branches giving way under the weight of snow but not due to the stress of the transition from hot to cool. Strangely enough it seems to be during the daylight hours that the branches fall, even on a still day, hence the name, as they have a way of dropping, with no apparent warning, on anyone who happens to be passing by.

I had no idea there could be so many different shades of green. Many years ago I remember a pretty little Irish song called 'Forty shades of green'. Well, move over Ireland, no one could count the different ones here. An English beechwood is a uniform pale green in spring, deepening to a lush, rich dark green as summer progresses. Autumn frosts turn the leaves to yellow, orange, red and brown; however, there is still an inherent uniformity. Here in my Patagonia not even one single tree is the same colour throughout. The older leaves are a muted grey-green. New growth is a mixture of dark red, emerald and yellow-green and countless shades between.

In early summer, the really big gums turn a hazy pale yellow as they come out in blossom. As these flowers dry and fall, they form a carpet everywhere, not just on the ground. They find their way into the cracks in the window ledges, among the cobwebs. They blow in through the screen door and create a yellow edge to the rug. Washing coming in from the clothesline has to be shaken out, as it has minute yellow strands stuck in every possible fold. Different trees have lovely crimson red blossoms and while the strands are rather longer they still find their way into everything. The difficulty becomes apparent if, like me, you like to walk about in bare feet. After the blossoms have fallen, the tiny gum nuts start to fall. Shaped like tiny acorn cups, they have needle-sharp points on the top. These are merciless and so easy to bring into the house stuck to the soles of shoes.

When it comes to resilience, my favourites are the wild flowers. After months of hardly any rain, come autumn and a hint of moisture, the tiniest flowers spring up out of the hard earth. How can anything so small and dainty possibly survive and thrive? Yet they do, with their tiny pink and yellow faces upturned to the sun.

I discovered the ruins of an old miner's cottage up in the sleeping-dragon hills. There were supposed to still be gold deposits to be found up there. I wondered if it was he or his wife who planted the roses, rosemary bushes and naked lady lilies. After nearly a century of neglect, the rose bush still sent forth beautiful, tiny pink roses. Too sophisticated to be the traditional hedge rose, but only just, and the perfume so sweet, nothing like carefully cultivated ones at all. The lilies fascinated me. Again after months of drought, as if by some hidden conductor's signal, up popped a single stem with anything up to a dozen pink flowers exploding from the top. After the flowers died off, then the thick, green leaves emerged. There seemed to be something upside down or back to front about that.

The hills, when carpeted in green grasses, looked serene and, as I said before, like a sleeping dragon. They were a mixture of gentle rolling slopes and steep escarpments. Sudden gullies and gorges cut through the red earth hillsides and it seemed to be on the steepest inclines that the gum trees grew. These weren't the majestic ones that stood in the garden and along the rivers. These were much smaller, their slender trunks reaching up perhaps thirty feet or more, and they were very supple and lissom. Like their big cousins, their bark stripped off in the blistering heat of summer and they were incredibly beautiful when covered in bright red and yellow gum flowers. Each different type had its own individual shape of gum nuts. I grew up with flower fairies. It was easy to imagine gum nut babies swinging aloft in those trees.

Beneath the trees were enormous, exposed boulders, coloured soft grey and covered in lichens of brilliant green, yellow and orange. The ground was covered in branches of all sizes and shapes and the curls of bark that had blown down. Being evergreens there were always leaves falling and resting wherever they landed. Set among the trees were countless small bushes. In the autumn they came alive with flowers of all colours, which inevitably brought a wealth of butterflies and moths in so many varied colours and types.

Unlike deciduous and rain forests, there was no canopy for protection. Despite there being millions of trees and shrubs, there was little solid shade. There was no absolute silence either. Always there was the sough of the breeze in the treetops, the call of songbirds and others of a more exotic heritage, the crack and rustle of some creature moving through the dried foliage. Life there was overflowing all the time regardless of the weather.

On the grassy hillsides, wild flowers soon withered in the sun and the rich green grasses passed from faded gold to palest yellow. Seed heads, having shed their kernels for another season, were almost transparent. Particularly in the dawn light, when the breezes chased across the hills, the hills become a sea of moving gold waves with silver tips and had a sound that made the hairs on one's arms stand up.

It is amidst this tranquillity that either the carelessness of man, or nature striking in the form of lightning, can cause a bushfire. Within seconds a tiny spark becomes a raging inferno. Dried grasses burn with amazing heat, the fire generates its own wind and suddenly the fire front is travelling at incredible speeds. This is bad enough in the grasslands, but if it spreads to the trees it will burn off thousands of hectares before slaving fire fighters can bring it under control. A phenomenon peculiar to gum trees, the resin rapidly heats up and literally explodes. Each tree becomes a blazing candle. The roiling heat tumbles about in the atmosphere forming fireballs that bounce across the treetops, igniting everything they touch, or race with extraordinary speed through the grass, spreading mayhem and destruction faster than the mind can comprehend. The flames are hard, red and orange, as incredibly intense in colour as heat, nothing at all like the cosy flames of the fire in the hearth. Thick, acrid smoke billows higher and higher. It has a clean smell somehow, not contaminated by chemicals and paint substances. This is a smell that strikes terror into the heart of anyone with any degree of sensitivity.

Once, a particularly bad fire occurred and the afternoon sun was turned into a blood-red ball and all plant life turned orange and gold. The next day, the worst of the fire had been extinguished. However, the pall of smoke lingered. Now the air was filled with ash and difficult to breathe. The morning sun was a silver ball and the foliage was blue.

Left behind in the fire's wake, the blackened earth and charred trees were as if stunned. Now there was silence. It was impossible to assess how many animals and birds had been destroyed; the fire burned with such intensity that not even bones remained. Yet out of that desolation, after some rain, new growth sprang forth. From those charred trees the smallest of green shoots pushed out and the bush quickly became once again a mass of new life surging towards the sun. The air was filled with birds singing and insects buzzing, life just getting on with being alive.

Seven

I had noticed while rambling around in my Patagonia that there were the most extraordinary geographical features.

In the south-east, near Mount Gambier, where the land is mostly flat or softly undulating and covered as far as the eye can see with pine forests, a volcano once erupted. Jutting abruptly up, it is almost perfectly cone-shaped. I clambered up to the top of the volcano and could see for goodness knows how many miles in every direction. I glimpsed the ocean too.

There are separate craters nestled in the bowl at the top of this extinct volcano. By following a winding track down in one, I came across two lakes. One of these is imaginatively called Brown Lake. Tourists have commandeered the lakes and ski boats could be seen screaming around their smooth surfaces. There is a carefully designed wooden walkway over the boggy places and between the reeds of the larger lake. The native birds and wildlife didn't appear to mind too much as I walked through their homeland. I didn't think it was very polite when a boat came zooming past. Of course the skier had to slant the skis to get around the bend and naturally the sheet of water they sent up saturated everyone on the walkway – including me.

The third crater holds a truly marvellous wonder, though very different, depending on what time of year you visit. Go there between, say, March and October and it is just your average, common or garden, standard-issue lake in a crater. It is reputed to be bottomless. Go there sometime between November and February and it is quite a different story. For a clue you could ask its name. You have it. The Blue Lake, and it really does change to the most amazing deep blue, regardless of how cloudy the skies are. I figure if you asked the lake what it wanted to be called, it would have chosen something much more imaginative than Blue Lake. No doubt the people indigenous to the area had a more poetic name.

I was told the whole area is riddled with all kinds of underground phenomena. Whoever would have thought, if you stepped a few paces to the side of the main street, you would find a large hole in the ground filled with dainty waterfalls, luxurious plant life and wonderful birds. In the grounds of one of the many timber mills in the region was an even larger hole, carved out by water somewhere over the millennia. This had been carefully nurtured so that it looked like a town park and gardens in miniature. It had its own lily ponds and goldfish, rose gardens, park benches and floodlights. There was a curtain of ivy trailing down some forty feet, which I could walk behind to get around the hollow.

Some distance away, much like the footbridge that took me to my Patagonia, there was a flight of concrete steps locked away behind a gate. Going down them was like stepping into another subterranean world. Stalagmites and stalactites frantically tried to reach each other between floor and ceiling, growing only one drip at a time and that not very often. (Now, do the 'tites have to be pulled up or do they fall down? Never could remember which. Hang on while I look it up... Stalactites come down. Well, I may remember for a couple of minutes. Probably not.) The stalactites came in stunning forms. Some were big and heavy conjuring up the deepest bass notes on a cathedral organ. Others so tiny and slender like icicles hanging from the eaves of a cottage, reminding me of Keats's 'Ode To Autumn', except he was referring to vines.

No matter how baking hot it is on the surface, the caves are always cool and damp. I went on guided tours down several of these caves. At one point the guide turned the lights off. Crikey O'Reilly, what an experience! We stood in darkness so dense it defied description. The silence was as oppressive as the sensation of tonnes of rock sitting above our heads. The collective sigh of relief when the lights were turned back on was clear evidence of how we all felt.

Not everyone holds the same views, however. I was not brave enough to investigate myself but I read brochures about other caves in the general area that are totally immersed in water. For a fee, and with some reasonable experience of underwater swimming and, as far as I was concerned, gigantic amounts of courage, people actually went exploring them.

It is not too far to the coast from the Blue Lake. There, a small community makes a living out of offshore fishing for crabs and crayfish.

The day I was there, all the boats were in the harbour because of the bad storm out to sea. The boats seemed to be so small to go out among the swelling waves and I had a fleeting and chilling awareness of the precariousness of their existence both literally and financially. I have the utmost admiration for anyone who is willing to go out to sea in a boat. While I love to splash around and float, I am not confident enough to be out of my depth. I need to know my feet can touch the bottom and my head is well clear of the water.

I fell in love with the lighthouse at Port MacDonnell. I rather fancied it as a place to live in. Nothing much between it and the Antarctic, and what a neighbour that would be. It added a whole new dimension to borrowing a cup of sugar. Just along from the lighthouse is a petrified forest. When the tide was out, I could see fossilised tree stumps and small fossilised branches glistening and flashing rainbows as the sun caught the multifaceted quartz.

I came across a little cove with virgin sand unsullied by human footsteps. For a moment, one could really imagine how it was before people came tramping around all over the place. Then, a quick and disappointing reality check as I saw a blue rubber sandal washed up behind a rock, and a cuttlebone that had someone's initials carved into it.

Travelling back north, the coast road took me past the Coorong. I would no doubt get into trouble with geologists but very simply it is a series of lakes that stretch for miles, separated from the great ocean by high sand dunes. The lakes rise and fall with the tide and are delicately pink under the summer sun.

At one point named Ninety Mile Beach – don't you just love those imaginative names for places? – I took my little car off the bitumen road. The signpost said I could take a four-wheel drive vehicle through there. I left my car in an area designated to tired vehicles.

It was another of those hiking affairs. The signpost said it was about one and a half kilometres to the ocean. OK, that wasn't too far. The sign didn't mention that I would be climbing up and down three rows of sand dunes and that the sand was very fine, causing my feet to sink, slip and slide with each step. It became very tiring after a while. Remembering to look up occasionally, I could see the ocean tempting and beckoning me on like a mysterious seducer.

As I stepped past the last lot of dunes, the beach stretched, as the name implied, for miles either way. The sand was harsh and gritty and much darker brown than the white dunes. Such a contrast. The beach was not very wide before gigantic, hungry waves came rolling and crashing in. I don't think they were delivering that cup of sugar from the Antarctic somehow. I had heard that sharks and the like came in quite close there. I wasn't going to find out.

I walked along the waterline and floundered trying to keep on my feet. Each receding wave felt like it was trying to drag the whole landmass back into the ocean with it. I wondered if the kangaroos or wallabies that had left their paw prints in the sand set up umbrellas and beach towels for a quiet afternoon in the sun. There was certainly no one else about. I rested for a while and soaked my senses in the enormousness and magnificence of the ocean before trudging back to the car. I savoured a cool drink and another quiet rest before setting off again.

For all that I mocked the name, that walk had the same effect as the high-walled gorge at Morialta Falls and the dolphin. It was good to be reminded of my lowly status in the face of Mother Nature's splendours.

Eight

Lake Alexandrina is north of the Coorong. It is the last resting place for the River Murray before it enters the ocean.

If I were an eagle soaring on high and looked down from my lofty viewing point, I would see how the great Murray River snakes across the land, or should that be through the land? It didn't get lost at all meandering through dense scrub where so many explorers and pioneers have become detached from their sense of reason and direction to wander aimlessly till exhaustion and dehydration peeled them from their mortal coil.

I went to the place where the Murray and the Darling rivers converge. I found a nice parking spot and walked over a small wooden bridge spanning a stream some fifteen feet wide. Yes, another of those Patagonian bridges; this one would have been flooded if the water rose about two feet, so I wasn't too worried. I followed a narrow pathway, keeping an eye out for snakes. An ideal spot for them, I would have thought. As I intrepidly – sounds grand – forged my way to the farthest end of the island, I could see the two rivers were on either side of me.

There was no big fanfare, no shaking of hands and loud hurrah when the two bodies of water met. Silently they flowed side by side, reluctant to mingle. How did I know this? Well, a bit later I read one of those information booths. It told me the Darling River is milky in colour because it has brought silt down with it from a billion miles away or Queensland, whichever is nearest. I could see the two very distinct flows, one green, the other milky. Only a short distance downstream, the weir sorted it all out. Whether they wanted to or not, they were all mixed up and came gushing and churning out the other side bubbling and frothing. Now were they pleased to be united like lost lovers – was that Cathy and Heathcliff I heard calling or did they just have to make the best of it like an arranged marriage?

Wherever this magnificent river runs, there are dead trees left in its wake. I don't know what happened to cause this. Perhaps I should find a botanically inclined friend rather than a nautical one for this problem. It looks like either the trees or the river didn't stick to an agreement, as trees, generally speaking, don't move about much once they have settled their roots. Yes, I know Tolkien's Ents do, but they are a little different. I reasoned it was the river that was fickle. Why else would so many dead trees be standing waist-deep in swirling waters? We are talking eucalyptus trees here too, which pride themselves on being quite capable of thriving on a teaspoon of water every few years. Well, a slight exaggeration perhaps. Anyway, they aren't like the weeping willows who always seem to have their feet standing in water and their skirts trailing in the current. So did the eucalypts die of waterloggeditis?

While my imagination was being challenged by this concept, I found a stretch of river where the land either side was so rich it had been cultivated for citrus fruits and grapes. What was this area called? The Riverland! I was amazed that people demonstrating staggering courage and endurance could minimise their achievements by such ordinary names. On second thoughts, it was that they were 'the common man' that made them so great and also made it easy to understand the simplicity of their naming techniques.

Driving through the area, I was intrigued by the signpost advertising the Tree of Knowledge. Now, who could resist that carrot? Not me, for sure. The road wound down to the riverbed and I found a caravan park. I was disconcerted, momentarily, by a statue of a pelican that dwarfed the kiosk. I was not entirely certain the look in its eye was welcoming. It would have been enough to frighten any self-respecting drunk on a moonlit night.

Eventually I found the Tree of Knowledge. Don't get too excited. It is a gum tree standing some distance from the river, and nailed to its trunk are plaques showing the height of the flood waters in different years. Not impressed? I confess I wasn't at first. Then I thought about it for a while. I realised it took quite a feat of imagination to picture all that lovely peaceful picnic area under fifteen or twenty feet of raging, muddy water, prepared to demolish and carry away anything that had the misfortune to get in the way.

Another one of those times when Mother Nature gave me a timely nudge back to the bottom of the humble ladder.

Nine

I heard someone say quite cryptically that doctors only become doctors so they don't have to write legibly like the rest of us. A bit harsh, I thought. However, one could wonder.

I recently had cause to visit a doctor and in turn was referred to the local hospital for an ultrasound. A little touch of irony when the radiologist had to telephone the doctor's rooms for a transcript of what was actually required. This time thing was interesting too, here in my Patagonia. I was warned this procedure would take up to an hour. No problem. And add a further half an hour, as I was to wait for the pictures to take with me. I thought this would be a good opportunity to brush up on the new Rules of the Road due to be implemented within a few days. This proved to be a slight miscalculation. The hour was accurate. However, the half turned out to be barely ten minutes. Sometimes it is difficult adjusting the allocated time to the actual.

This was a lot like watching the sun set. The weatherman on the radio told me every day at what precise moment the sun would set. He didn't tell me I needed to allow anything up to two hours for this remarkable event if I really wanted to see the full glory. Especially if watching by the ocean.

About half an hour or so before the time the sun would set, everything began to change. The atmosphere quietened and harsh clarity toned down. Even with a sea breeze, everything seemed still and paused, waiting. Birds called in muted voices as they prepared to settle for the night. The blue of the eastern sky had already begun to darken imperceptibly.

I liked it best when there were clouds. They seemed to come from nowhere as if they knew their presence would add even more glory. They were certainly correct in that assessment. I mentioned this to someone once and they helpfully explained about the change in air temperature causing condensation. All very logical. I prefer the idea of clouds wanting to make the whole affair as glamorous and glorious as possible.

The clouds appeared as enormous, white billowing masses, yet when the sun's rays pierced them they were grey with an underskirt of silver, and all the different height layers became apparent. As the sun lowered, the silver turned to molten gold and some of the grey turned to cream. There was a pathway of gold lying across the ocean that shone on every tiny ripple.

The gulls started flying north, as solitary individuals or in small flocks. They glided low over the water as stark black silhouettes. One time, a snowy white gull came quite close to me and just for a fragment of time became completely golden. I remember thinking that if I were to lose my sight, what a perfect final image that would be.

Everything seemed to stop, as the fiery disk of the sun sank gracefully into the ocean.

Now the real art show began that too few people wait for. The afterglow. At first it was as if the sky was in a state of disbelief: where had the sun gone? Then the place above where it was last seen lit up with a subtle brilliance that was heartbreakingly lovely, lasting such a brief time it seemed to echo the thought 'Please don't go.' As if to assist the mind to accept the inevitable loss, the sky turned a miraculous array of crimsons and then faded slowly through a multitude of dusky pinks and apricots. At this moment, I have seen the tiniest sickle of a new moon, blood red, as if newborn, with the gallant Dog Star in attendance. Another time when I turned away from the western skies to the east, I saw the full moon floating over the hills like a perfect orange ball, a muted reflection of the sun that had just left my field of vision.

As my eyes adjusted to the fading light, the darkened sky became dotted with twinkling stars. They looked so shy in those early hours, yet as the night settled they filled the heavens with blazing assurance. Small wonder we have been known to console ourselves that our beloved dead become stars watching over us.

I remember in the 1980s when Halley's Comet came to visit. My son dragged me out to the garden, where I dutifully agreed that among that dazzling display of stars and haze of course I could see the comet and its tails. I hadn't the heart to say I couldn't really distinguish one lot from the rest, yet, if asked, I say I was a witness.

When I have read of lemon-coloured skies, I have thought, 'Oh yeah.'

One morning I watched the sunrise from beside the Port River where it flows into the sea. The land is rough and pretty much as originally made with small clumps of bushes and tiny wild flowers. The sky really was lemon-coloured and a passing shower had washed the colour out of the new sun so it shone watery, white gold, before seeking refuge among some clouds. It turned the river into a liquid mirror and filled the raindrops on the car window with rainbows.

Remember I spoke of the moon that looked like an orange lantern? The next morning I watched as it turned into silver tissue paper and disappeared into blue clouds while the sun appeared in the eastern sky amid swaths of candy-floss-pink clouds. I don't believe there was an artist's palette capable of re-creating the colours I have seen in the sunrises and sunsets, and certainly words do a very poor job. Perhaps it was like the waterfall: you just had to get out there and look for yourself. My Patagonia is like that. Just allow plenty of time.

Ten

I was sitting in my cosy lounge one evening and heard single taps on the tin roof of the balcony. I was a bit slow identifying them as raindrops till there could be no mistaking the drumming they grew in to. Out of the night sky, the wind started howling. The windows rattled alarmingly and the gum trees began thrashing about as if demon-possessed. The noise became so loud it was impossible to hear the music I had been enjoying. I had no choice other than to turn it off. Rain lashed the windows and I could hear a torrent of water gushing from the gutters. The darkness was savagely split by javelins of blue lightning, being hurled at the earth by an angry, unseen hand. Thunder rolled and roiled over the roof making me cringe in my chair, fearful I would be squashed under the weight of the sound.

Eventually the storm blew itself out or it just decided to visit another neighbourhood. Mother Nature knocked out an electricity power plant and our world went very dark. Candlelight was so kind.

I turned my hand to candle making once. I bought a starter kit. The instructions were a bit of a challenge. I dutifully ate baked beans on toast for lunch so I could use the empty can to melt my wax in. I didn't fancy using the saucepan that I was going to cook my dinner in later. The instructions didn't give me useful information like how much wax you need to melt to fill the appropriate container. I hadn't realised that fat candles burn in the middle, leaving a hollow shell. Much like a newly made bread roll when you pull out the soft fluffy dough from the middle and leave just the crust.

I now had a number of these hollow candles. One day I might try melting them down again and making tall thin ones. Why would someone want to make candles with holes in the middle? Some trick to do with putting ice cubes in the mould and then pouring hot wax on and the candle sets with holes in. I kept getting confused with that Swiss cheese that was all holes and made me wonder if a little person had been harmlessly blowing bubbles somewhere before getting rained on by liquid cheese.

Talking of rain, as we were, after that storm I went to sleep. The next morning when I awoke I couldn't work out what the unusual sound was. I had grown accustomed to the silence disturbed only by the croaking of frogs and an assortment of waterfowl who always seemed to have something to say. I wandered to the kitchen to look out of the window. Was I surprised! The growling roar filling the atmosphere was coming from the river. A raging animal filled the riverbed and in some places lapped the very brink. Gone the little trickle, bumbling along to the next pond. Now unrelenting ferocity fought to escape its confines. The reeds that normally stood to attention even under the most gruelling heat were all leaning over desperately hanging on. Not so lucky were some great branches and assorted debris that went swooshing past.

On and off throughout the morning I watched in fascination as the river kept rising. Just at the bottom of the steps beside the house, it finally broke the bank and a pond quickly formed where the day before had been a pretty grassy area, ideal for a picnic. I smiled at a couple of ducks that flew in and decided this pool was preferable to the river. I considered this a definite sign of intelligence. I couldn't believe that, violent as the storm felt to me, it could have rained that much for the river to be so changed. Curiosity won. In hindsight, it was stupid to do the tourist thing. The roads were covered with all kinds of fallen trees and detritus and the Emergency Services people were fully occupied keeping up with the calls for assistance. I passed a ford where a vehicle had been washed into the river. The driver had been able to free himself from the inside and was stranded on the roof. A team of hard-working men were setting up a system of ropes and pulleys to drag the vehicle and its hapless driver out. When I passed by much later, the man was gone but the vehicle was still there, submerged even lower under the hungry waters. It stayed there for several days.

Meanwhile, I continued along the twisting, turning, narrow road that took me up into the hills. I said they looked like a sleeping dragon. That was certainly true from a distance. In amongst them was a different story all together. Great walls of rock soared either side of the road, all seeping moisture. Some areas just a wet sheen, in others little rivulets had formed, developing into small, but fast-flowing waterfalls. Everything was dripping and wet and flowing towards the lowest level. It's a tribute to man's ingenuity and resilience when they were confronted with the task of blasting and digging out a place for the road through those impassive rock masses.

Another such testament is the Kangaroo Dam. When the water level is down, it looks like the sides of a giant teacup holding the water back. The whole area known as the Chain of Ponds is an enormous natural water catchment system. So much rain had fallen over the hills during the night that water in the dam had become dangerously high and the overflow floodgates had been opened. If I thought the river by the house looked fierce, then my eyes were now being opened much wider. It is impossible to describe the sheer magnitude and power as billions of litres of suppressed water strained to be free. The noise was unbelievable. It was an absolute onslaught on my senses. The road was beginning to become congested with other carloads of people doing exactly what I was doing, so I drove on out of everyone's way.

I went on to explore the Chain of Ponds. Seen now, after the storm, they brooded under heavily clouded skies. The wind had whipped up little white-capped wavelets all across the surface, which reached high up to the tree line. This was an encouraging sight as the water would be needed to supply the city and suburbs throughout the long, hot summer to come. In the early light of a still day, they lay dark green with barely a ripple. As the sky lightened, the blue reflected on the water. Surrounding tall, dark pine trees, richly green, make the area look like the picturesque scene on a chocolate box – all that is missing is the Swiss chalet. Mostly they are edged with native eucalypts. When the cream, yellow and red blossoms are in flower, the pollen falls and become a haze of colour on the surface. It was an enchanting sight to see a black swan gliding over the water leaving behind a perfect arrow in its wake. Yes, a lot like the water rat but this was more conventionally aesthetic.

As the water level drops, the shallow banks of the reservoirs turn emerald green as new grasses spring up. Then, as summer sets in, the grasses scorch and dry, the banks become bare, cracked, red earth again. Under the constant glare of the sun, the waters evaporate and are watched with mounting anxiety. I saw them once, vast hollows empty of all water except a narrow stream that had cut a deep, zigzagging channel for itself.

I had visions of it burrowing underground in order to survive. Was it a fact or a figment of my imagination that even on the hottest of days, the air was cooler as I drove through the Chain of Ponds?

While my little river was still running high, a number of vehicles turned up at the bottom of the garden. To my surprise, several canoes were unloaded and placed in the swirling waters. In a twinkling they were barrelling along and lost to sight. Not quite shooting the white water rapids of the Zambezi but satisfying for the canoeists, I suppose.

After several days, the river had returned to normal size. The reeds dried out and gradually sprang back upright. The trees that insisted on growing in the river bed stayed bent over, weighed down by litter and sodden vegetation clinging tenaciously to anything available. I thought of all those creatures that make the riverbank their home. A good spring clean was always desirable but being flushed out to this extent was rather extreme. The casualties must have been horrendous.

Eleven

On another occasion, I set off in a northerly direction, then did a sharp left and left again. This brought me to the Yorke Peninsula. Part of the wheat belt, there were miles and miles of rolling hills, gleaming faded gold in the early summer light. Nothing like the pocket-handkerchief-sized fields I knew as an English farmer's daughter, with their comfortable hedges and masses of wild flowers sprinkled among the corn.

The ground was thickly interspersed with rocks of all sizes, there appeared to be no creeks running, yet here the grain grew magnificently. I arrived during harvest time. Combine harvesters with a cutting blade twice the width of the ones I recalled laboured across these vast acres. Instead of the grain being bagged on the harvester, it poured like golden rain from a chute directly into the truck being driven alongside.

Perhaps the most amazing thing for me was to see the lines of trucks, all kinds, sizes and vintages, with great mounds of grain covered by tarpaulins, patiently waiting to go over the weighbridge, before unloading the grain into the enormous silos.

The peninsula is only a narrow tract of land and the sea must have been very deep immediately offshore, as great ships came in to take the grain away. Ardrossan had a long jetty reaching out into the sea where the ships used to come in. There was still a disused railway line running along its length; surely it would have many and varied tales to tell if it could talk. It was silent the day I was there. In fact, everything seemed silent. The jetty was littered with the debris of enthusiastic fishermen and I watched my first squid being caught.

The water itself was the darkest green, reminding me of the colour of pine trees. The cliffs were rich, brick-red and pitted with holes, large enough for a flock of pigeons to make their homes in. I stood at the end of the jetty facing south. I watched a pearly-pink full moon rise over the mainland on one side and the brilliant golden ball of the setting sun on the other.

Right at the bottom end of the peninsula, protected as part of a national park, is a place called Pondalowie. Lovely name, isn't it? To get there, I drove along a dirt track between bright white sand dunes. There were breaks between the dunes revealing seascapes that defy description. Like waterfalls, you have to go and have a look for yourself.

I had to pull over and wait while a family of emus crossed the road. The adult emu was surrounded by eight or nine inquisitive miniature replicas of itself, the whole family looking remarkably like overgrown chickens.

There is a small, sheltered bay here for yachts to berth. It is the perfect picture of a quiet, peaceful, safe haven. Either side of the mouth of the bay are staggering cliffs. The ocean surges in, heaving and rolling like a sleeping giant turning over under the bedclothes. The water is incredible shades of pale green and blue, to the deepest blue I have ever seen. When I was there, it was covered in a fragile tracery of white foam like spiders' webs. The waves pound off the cliff faces and have eroded and hollowed them so they have gigantic overhanging pieces that are quite unsafe to walk on. Apart from the natural beauty of the place, it is quite well known for the quality of the surf. I could not imagine anyone surfing those waves; it's that feet of clay thing again. I left there quite stunned by the sight and sound of that secluded piece of paradise.

I loved the small country towns. They all had wide main streets, often with a grassed nature strip down the centre. I found far too many war memorials, naming the young men who had gone to war and not returned. They spoke volumes of the farming families who would have been devastated by the absence of the next generation to take over. There was an abundance of well-tended memorial gardens around them and even a bandstand or two.

The buildings all seemed to be of a similar era and typically colonial, with the standard issue town hall or Masonic hall and churches of different denomination. The churches were so small, with an air of permanence about them. Each one had its own cemetery, many of the names and poetic inscriptions on the gravestones so worn by wind and weather as to be almost unreadable. They retained a reverent dignity that wasn't sensed quite the same in the newer cemeteries.

There was also a great sense of pride in the gardens everywhere, with all kinds of unexpected things converted to something picturesque. Two that came to mind with little hesitation were the porcelain toilet bowl, sitting at the end of a drive, painted leaf green and overflowing with red flowering geraniums. The second was a tree stump some four feet high with a lawnmower, painted pale pink, somehow anchored on at an angle to show it off to perfection. These were demonstrations of a wry sense of humour.

Moonta had a fascinating sweet shop. It was housed in a tiny building and protected like an endangered species. Inside were row upon row of glass jars displaying a fabulous array of old-fashioned, shiny boiled sweets plus some newer varieties to cater for all tastes.

The less amusing side was the air of desolation that surrounded other landmarks. Monuments to the intrepid spirit of those early pioneers are the stone cottages. Like something created by a child, these cottages are plain, small oblong boxes, with windows like blind eyes, staring vacantly out onto the stark landscape. All those rocks scattered in the paddocks are what is left after someone painstakingly gathered hundreds and hundreds of them to build solid walls about a foot thick to protect their families from heat and wind.

Whatever criterion did they use to choose one spot over another? There were few trees and even fewer creeks. Wells or bores must have been dug for water and it was beyond my imagination to re-create the harsh conditions and soul-destroying hard work needed to scratch a meagre survival. Where had the families gone, leaving their homes to fall down and become silhouettes of stolid simplicity against a clear blue sky? There must have been a terrible link between those deserted homes and the names on the war memorials.

As always with nature, there is a balance. The fantastic rock formations off the coastline that looked so photographable also brought catastrophe to hundreds of ships. The rusted hulls of several could still be seen on the beaches. At an information booth I found a map with the offshore sites marked, the final resting place of ships, crew and passengers. It was hard to reconcile that majestic beauty with such bitter tragedy.

Twelve

Having already established my reluctance to go far into the water, I consider it a major personal achievement to have taken the ferry to Kangaroo Island. It's that name thing again. It popped up a lot on the journey over. Nautically minded people have told me it is wonderful to sail a yacht in the waters from either Yorke Peninsula or even Port Adelaide over to Kangaroo Island. I don't raise even an eyebrow in question of the validity of their assertions. Just the very thought leaves me shuddering – certainly not in distaste, more those feet of clay I have clumping firmly on land, reminding me where they rightfully belong.

Getting out of bed at four in the morning was the start of my trip to the island. I had to drive south, a bit over a hundred kilometres to Cape Jervis. Even allowing it was before six when I arrived, there seemed to be very little there other than a handful of houses.

First big challenge – to drive the car onto the ferry! It really was very difficult if all your instincts were yelling, 'Close your eyes.' From my point of view, never mind economics, too many cars were being herded into the deep, dark bowels of the ship. Oh, all right! So it was just a small boat, really; it just seemed like a long way down. Once my car was safely tucked in, I went up onto the deck. This was much, much better!

The ocean was superb, very picturesque with endless little waves all capped in snowy white lace. The ferry seemed to skim with amazing ease over the tops. I wasn't too fussed whether this was considered a calm crossing or not. I remember being taken in by that line thirty-odd years before when taking the Liverpool to Dublin ferry. To seasoned travellers it may have been the calmest crossing in a million years, but that didn't stop me throwing up for eight hours. I even lost a quarter of an inch off my not very tall height.

Was I ready for the name thing? We were crossing Backstairs Passage. Now doesn't that conjure up all kinds of illicit goings-on? At the very least, pirates, smuggling or visits to ladies of the night. Actually, it was the whalers who put this whole area on the map, with or without notoriety. The skipper of the ferry (I wonder if that should be captain? I was trying to be nautical) said that if we watched carefully we might see dolphins. They liked to ride shotgun, playing chasing games among the wake. It was a wonderful distraction looking for them and the water spraying off the sides of the ferry was very pretty. However, it didn't take long for me to feel decidedly off-colour. Someone kindly suggested I go down below and have a cuppa. It was a nice enough arrangement down there, tables with edges to stop the crockery falling off in rough weather, but the very fact the tables and benches were bolted to the deck I found disconcerting. I went back upstairs where the fresh wind was much better than the closed-in warmth below. How glad I was that the trip only took an hour.

I was quite proud of myself driving the car off the ferry back onto dry land with sighs of relief. It was another drive of some seventy kilometres to get to Kingscote, where I was booked into a cabin on a caravan park next to the sea. Kingscote is much like all other small country towns and an information brochure told me that in the evening large numbers of fairy penguins would come to stay the night among the rocks. Sounded good to me. I sat by the jetty eating fish and chips out of their paper wrapping surrounded by aggressive seagulls. The sun went down and I snuggled up in my coat, torch ready, and waited, and waited and waited. It was very dark when I gave up and walked along the narrow strip of sand. I stopped short when I heard a funny sound. I won't even attempt to describe it. Enough to say I managed to track it down and there amongst the rocks was one, solitary and very lonely-looking fairy penguin. He or she was lovely.

I had heard a lot about and seen many pictures of the Remarkable Rocks. Yes, it's that name thing again. I was a bit sceptical about what I would really find as I braved the winding dirt track through the trees that hid everything from view. I even thought of giving up all together a couple of times when large tourist buses came trundling through and didn't seem to give me much time to get out of their way. But I persevered and as I clambered from my car to the rocks, I was stunned and could only mutter, 'They really are remarkable.' Like the cliffs at Pondalowie, the wind and rain has done a magnificent job hollowing out those enormous boulders. I just couldn't understand how they could stay so precariously balanced on each other, perched so high with no protection at all from the elements.

Next I forged my intrepid way to Seal Bay. Well, I felt intrepid going along what felt like endless dirt roads with no company except the invisible bird whose startling calls I could hear. By that time, I had stopped getting upset about names because one look down onto the bay made it quite clear why it was called Seal Bay. As part of a guided tour, I was escorted among seals of all ages and temperaments. I didn't need reminding not to get too close to any of them; the big males were seriously scary. The babies were simply enchanting. I could have stayed forever watching them basking on the beach and marvelling at the contrast as they bounced inelegantly to the water where they swam and surfed with indescribable grace in the surging tide. Yes, it is another of those 'beyond words' experiences that you just have to go and see for yourself.

American River gave me my first encounter with pelicans up close. Every afternoon at three o'clock was feeding time. A couple had started doing this as a way of ensuring that injured pelicans would stay alive. As it was pointed out to us, terrible damage is done when unsuspecting pelicans get tangled up in fishing line. They literally starve to death. It didn't take long for word to get about amongst the pelicans and not just the injured ones had an afternoon snack, but it was touching to note that the lady dishing out the fish heads and guts made a point of reaching those who were injured. She even had names for some of them and Jonathon was the one that had started all of this. Of course, where there are fish, the seagulls are never far away. There were warning signs to be aware that seagulls were not backward in coming forward in grabbing food from anyone's hand. I was really frightened when I felt the strength in their wings as they hovered over my head and I made contact with their gimlet eyes.

Eventually it was time to return to the mainland. Driving the car onto the ferry and parking it was nowhere near as traumatic as driving on and I went up onto the deck sort of looking forward to the sea crossing. It seemed awfully choppy to me and the captain did mention that he was racing an oncoming storm. My heart sank down into my sandals straight away but then someone called out that they had spotted dolphins. Well, that improved things no end. I won't go so far as to say I didn't feel seasick, but certainly watching dolphins playing in the waves created by the boat kept me distracted.

Epilogue

It didn't take twenty-six hours of plane travel bringing me halfway across the world to open my eyes more to the unique place that is South Australia. It took a walk across a wobbly foot suspension bridge on a sunny afternoon...

When I have talked to people about things I have seen in my ramblings here, I felt I might just as well have been talking about the real Patagonia. I have been astonished and somewhat dismayed how little people have looked around them. Often it was those same people who scrimped and saved so they could travel overseas to Europe, America and Asia who seemed to have the least idea about the world outside their own back door; the ever-present wonders of nature and the tributes to the makers of our history.

I have said several times that some things you just have to get out and see for yourself. I believe that is true for everything. No amount of clever words, photographs, movies or paintings will replace the personal experience of watching a sunset, climbing even a small mountain or going across a bridge and looking at the world with a different set of eyes.

Down by the River

Introduction

Here I sit in my studio. It's a wonder I get any writing done at all as I'm constantly being distracted by the view from my big window with its glass sliding door onto the balcony. I am no longer living in the foothills, surrounded by trees. I am no longer alone.

I have never wanted to buy a house. Something in me wanted to be able to pack a suitcase and be gone at a moment's notice. In 2001 I was living alone in my rented tree house. I didn't even have a tenancy agreement after the first year, so was able to give two weeks' notice when it came time to leave.

The tree house had been called that because it nestled on a hillside overlooking a small river, and the tall gum trees towered over the roof, giving the impression that I was living in the trees. The river became little more than a series of ponds if the summer was very dry and could turn into a raging torrent overnight when it rained heavily in the hills and the run-off raced down to the distant sea. I could look out of my window straight into the eyes of a koala or an owl and I shared my garden with echidnas and blue-tongue lizards. I watched the sun rise over the hills, enthralled as it sent long fingers of light along the river valley, turning the treetops down there to gold. Through an arched window I watched the setting sun paint the western sky with fire. All year round, during the daylight hours, with varying degrees of density, my tree house was filled with green light.

Some years ago, I was going through a very unhappy time and decided to create, in writing, Brenda's Dream House. I went out and bought an A4-size hardback notebook with the Edith Holden *Diary of an Edwardian Lady* dog-rose picture on the cover. My house was going to suit me and would have nothing to do with reality.

As I sat down to write, I found I was starting by asking where in the world I wanted the house to be. The answer was here in Australia.

I had such pleasure designing the house and garden. I wanted the house to be on a swivel base so I could turn it to have the sun coming into the kitchen window at breakfast time and again when I was preparing an evening meal. I also wanted underground heating so I could have polished floorboards and natural slate tiles with a few rugs about and still be warm.

What was more revealing, I created a way of life too. I have always wanted to share my life with a like-minded person who had similar interests – a love of words, art, music, old movies and nature. I created a circle of fictitious friends who came for meals and we had lively conversations with plenty of laughter.

Ten years later, I found myself reaching for the same book and this time I wrote about a real house that is home for a dream come true.

Moving in

Stephen and I had only known each other a few weeks when we decided it was foolish for both of us to pay individual rents. Stephen's current lease was coming to an end and he enjoyed living in Port Adelaide and I loved the idea of being close to the beach, so we set about searching for somewhere to share. My sons were initially taken aback by this decision, especially as I had been living alone for the previous ten years.

My youngest (then thirty years old) put on his paternalistic attitude and asked carefully if I was sure I knew what I was doing.

My answer was 'You know the saying be careful what you wish for, you might get it? Well, I wished for and I got it.'

With that he shrugged and said, 'That's all right then. Do you need help moving?'

Stephen's son was harder to convince and it took some months before he relaxed a bit and could see I wasn't about to take advantage of his dad and that I did make him happy.

Amazingly we quickly found this house and as soon as we stepped into the living area we knew it had been waiting for us to come along. It certainly didn't hurt our chances that I had been in the tree house for eighteen years and worked for the government for over twenty years and Stephen owned his own publishing business. We looked what we were: a middle-aged professional couple and a good risk for the estate agent.

Stephen had a town house full of furniture and literally hundreds of books that make up his personal library. I had a small house full of furniture. Our choices in belongings were quite different. I had varnished pine bookcases, a round pine table and chairs and my new lounge suite was pale green and blue chintz-look with a medallion rug in similar shades. Stephen had very modern leather chairs and a leather two-seater couch. All his books lived in white sleek bookcases and his dining table was rectangular with chrome legs and wood top. It's strange that when he first took me to his house I was struck by the serenity of the clean lines and the white and cream furniture but the first thing I did was ask where the colours were. Before long he had splashes of red and yellow about the place with cushions and flowers.

The challenge now was how to blend these styles into one house. My three sons rallied and it was arranged they would all come with trailers and move our large furniture pieces in the one evening. The night was hot, sticky and raining. The next slight hitch was that my eldest son had to pull out at the last minute as his wife had gone into labour. I moved into a new life and had another new grandson (my fifth) all in one day.

I suppose it's here I must explain that the tree house was set well below road level and the drive was short, steep and curved, which meant the furniture had to be carried up the drive to the trailers parked on the road. I find myself cringing even more as I confess that Stephen's town house had three storeys with a narrow winding staircase. We were not going to be the easiest of removal jobs.

Anyway, it can be said that over several hours and with our fleet of cars and trailers and strong arms we moved all the large furniture. It was a case of that bed and chest of drawers upstairs in the master bedroom and that bed in the guest bedroom; those bookcases upstairs in the studio. We paused and pondered what we were going to do with all the lounge furniture.

Our living area is a very spacious square and as you enter it, the kitchen area is to the left with a wrap-around bar to separate it from the rest. So it was decided the chintz suite would go in front of the kitchen area. With the settee against the wall and the chairs opposite with their backs to the rest of the room we have what one of my sons called 'the cosy corner'. It is the corner everyone gravitates to and the name has stuck. My copy of a Hans Heysen painting of his wife sitting sewing by an open window looks very well on the wall behind the settee.

There is a large alcove to the right of the entrance where the television was set up so, naturally, Stephen's modern lounge furniture went in there. This left the far corner for Stephen's dining table.

It is incredible to me how well it all blended in. The whole house is fitted with blue carpet which we don't particularly like but we have managed to cover it with an assortment of coloured rugs.

It was late when the boys left and my middle son did the Old Father Time thing. He assured us that before the weekend was over we would have an argument but not to worry as things would all work out; just be patient. His concern was heart-warming, but several years have gone and we're still waiting for the argument.

Immediately inside the front door to the left is Stephen's office. I think it was intended to be used as a formal dining room but it's perfect for Stephen to run the business from. Visitors are fascinated by the computers and banks of printers that are used to keep it all ticking over. Even now if I go downstairs in the middle of the night I'm bemused by the several different colour stand-by lights that are always on.

I had taken a week off work, which I used to shunt the rest of my belongings down to the river house. It's funny the things we throw away when we move. I'm not much of a hoarder but even so I found myself being quite ruthless about the things I wanted to keep. It was strange going to the dump with the bits and pieces that were going to remain in my past. I hadn't realised how many pot plants I had accumulated either.

I was still cleaning out the kitchen cupboards which I had left till last, when the doorbell rang. I was horrified to see an estate agent there with two couples who were interested in buying the place. I felt betrayed by my landlord, as he had not said anything to me about this. Perhaps he thought I would be at work and no one would know. Either way it spoiled a good relationship that had lasted for the eighteen years I had enjoyed living in the tree house.

I finished the final clean-up and drove away for the last time. It was a wrench and I shed quite a few tears saying goodbye to memories. But I had a new life waiting for me. At fifty-nine, I had given up hope of such a thing happening.

Stephen spent that time moving box after box of his books into the river house and loading them up on shelves. This was an enormous task. I think in some ways it must have been as hard for him, as he had only moved from Canberra a year before to start a new life. He had barely made his new place his home before he had to pack up all his new things and move again. But like me he was looking forward to an unexpected future full of promise.

While living in the tree house, I had taken the bus daily to work from the north-eastern suburbs into Adelaide city. It felt so strange having to get up early to catch the train into the city. But one of the sweetest things was having Stephen walk me to the train station. At the end of the working day I trotted back to the train and, sure enough, there was Stephen waiting for me to get off. I loved the walk back home taking the path beside the canal that turns in a right angle at the end of the tidal reach. Walking round that sharp bend was like stepping from one world into another.

Because I had lived alone for so long, I was concerned that I would find adjusting to a lack of solitude difficult. Stephen made this so easy. When I first came home, I went upstairs to my studio. Stephen does most of the cooking in our house and I would come down when I heard him pottering around in the kitchen. Just this short while of transition was wonderful.

A while ago, I retired and now I spend most of my days in my studio reading or writing or helping to prepare manuscripts for printing and watching the tidal reach while Stephen works downstairs. We are each alone but together. A very undemanding and satisfying arrangement.

A room with a view

As a girl growing up in England, living in a very old farmhouse, I wanted one day to live in a bungalow. For almost forty years here in Australia this is what I have done. Now I live in a two-storey house again and I'm still paying rent. After several years I still get a thrill from climbing the stairs to go to bed and often recall the candle I carried to light my way as a young girl.

Downstairs in the cosy corner is a narrow white bookcase. Sitting on top is a small white table lamp, an elegant vase with two yellow silk poppies, a peach-pink crystal bud vase, and a small crystal bell with a delicate chime. Last is Darling. She is a Royal Doulton figurine; the original had been designed and made for Queen Mary in the 1920s. My Darling was a gift from a friend of my mother's in England who had never married (I believe her fiancé was killed in the Battle of Britain). She wrapped the figurine up with such care to send her winging across the world. I look at Darling with her slightly bent head, the almost boyish short hair, and long white nightdress, and the child within is touched and reminded of the sense of utter safety my parents gifted me so many years ago. More poignant perhaps because since living here I am experiencing that same sense of security.

Now in my sixties and well into retirement, I spend most of my days upstairs in my studio. This gives me the solitude I need. But I draw comfort from the knowledge that Stephen is downstairs in his office doing what he loves – editing and publishing books. The whole house is peaceful and quiet. Stephen likes to have classical music playing softly. I prefer silence. I suppose it is the silence that you get in the country with the constant sound of the wind and birdsong.

It took a year or more to get used to not having trees close by to limit my view of the sky. I felt exposed and vulnerable as great cloud banks rolled in off the sea and an invisible hand painted panoramic sunsets rich with red and gold clouds. Now I also have vast and spectacular views of the dawn sky from the guest bedroom window. I can see the hills where I used to live and I watch mesmerised most mornings as the sky brightens and eventually the sun rises. I bask in feelings as primitive as any sun-worshipper of thousands of years ago. I have discovered that when the sky is overcast I feel a similar sensation as when surrounded by very tall trees. For a while, it is a relief from all that vastness.

My studio is home for the many thousands of words I have written as poems or stories over the years. While it's true I started handwriting these mental meanderings, I now use a computer to be sure other people can read what I have written. But I don't trust it not to eat my work, so everything over the years has been printed off and stored in folders in a bookcase beside my other desk.

How rich am I to have two desks! I have folders of photographs from my childhood and when my own children were growing up. My other desk is white, which is probably a mistake because this is where I do my artwork. I notice the desktop is smeared with purple paint and green ink at the moment. No doubt one day I shall get enthusiastic and clean it off.

The tall bookcase that came with me from the tree house holds old friends and in the literature section are the books of poetry I have had published. Another dream come true. I run my eyes over the titles on the shelves and I am instantly taken back to when I read them – especially the textbooks from when I went to college aged thirty-five to do adult matriculation. I found I wasn't able to combine running a home of six people with studying full-time and had to stop halfway through. It was difficult writing essays while doing the washing and ironing! But even in that short time I became aware that I knew more than I realised about a lot of things and that gave me enormous confidence in my own potential other than being a homemaker and a mother, much as I loved being both.

There is another bookcase that holds the novels, mostly discovered initially in the library during the years when there was no money to buy books, and later found in second-hand book shops. I have newly acquired books of Australian history and literature. After all these years of living here in Australia, I have finally found an interest in Australian writers. I have spent such lovely hours browsing through second-hand book shops in search of the writers of the mid-1900s. Years ago I had read a number of books about the early settlement years and the horrible accounts of the plight of the convicts and eventually lost interest. They all seemed to be so similar. Then I read one of the new books Stephen was publishing, set in Queensland, and suddenly it was if someone had opened a window in my mind. Stephen then introduced me to Xavier Herbert's *Capricornia* and *Poor Fellow My Country*. They were challenging in every sense, especially learning more about the treatment of Aborigines, but I am so glad I have discovered such a wealth of information about the country I have called home for so long.

While I was at college, I started reading the poems of Bruce Dawe. I already knew I didn't really like the style of Lawson and Paterson, but Dawe's poems were different. In 2009 we went to Brisbane to be part of the launch of a biography of Bruce Dawe that Stephen had published and we met the man himself. Sitting around a table having coffee before the launch, I discovered he was such an interesting man and a born storyteller. Later, when he read some of his own work for us, he brought it to life in a way no one else could have done. I have learned that this is so often the case.

Sometimes I think my mind will explode with too many words that I have read or want to write and I know it's time to do something different. I make no claim to be an artist, but I do love to paint sea, sky and landscapes. My pictures are littered about my studio and hold me in an embrace it is hard to describe. Again, each time I look at them, I am transported back to the time I painted them, reliving the sense of walking away and just being in the place I am painting.

For the past ten years or so, I have kept pictorial diaries. I have used hardcover A4 books with plain pages and painted a backdrop taking great care with the colour of the mood I was in. Then I would write out the thoughts and feelings as I struggled to come to terms with some of the harsher realities of life. I foraged in newsagents and art supplies stores to find a wonderful assortment of gel pens, some that sparkled and some that even left a rainbow effect. Some of the writings might be a bit hard to read especially when for a period I had to use my left hand – I broke my right wrist tripping over a kerb in the car park after going to the cinema to see one of the Harry Potter movies. I suppose I've come a long way, as the latest diary has the picture on one page and a poem on the page next to it and is much easier to read. In this diary I simply record the lovely things in my life, like tomatoes and cucumbers growing in the garden.

I have always been a nature child and evidence of this is clear in my studio. For a time, one wall was covered with bamboo 'fencing'. I often see it in people's gardens to hide a boring metal fence. I had it so I could hang photographs of birds and so on, plus strings of seashells and wooden beads and paper flowers…

Nothing stands still and even since I began writing this, two new bookcases have been installed along the nature wall. My personal library continues to grow.

It's strange how, when given the opportunity, we discover hidden things inside us. For many years I had wanted a roll-top bureau with little cubbyholes to place papers and things in. For years I did own one but when I moved in with Stephen it didn't seem right to bring what had been a gift from my children's father. My youngest son has now given it a home. But I found I still like the concept of cubbyholes for things. Stephen and I found this super storage unit, thanks to Ikea, and the different-size spaces hold a range of boxes – no two alike, I must say – to hoard art supplies, paper, craft things even a sewing box. On the top sits the printer, a maidenhair fern and a lacquered bowl filled with stones and a little pagoda in the middle to hold incense sticks.

I'm beginning to wonder if I'm a more private person than I was aware. In writing about the contents of my studio, I see how much it reflects me. Again it is time to come clean. Sitting unobtrusively beside my desk is a small wooden chest. It's the old-fashioned kind with the rounded lid and fancy metal handles at each end. I painted it a mottled maroon, leaving a central panel of pale green with red and cream roses. I used old-gold paint to highlight the borders. Inside is my own treasure trove. It must be thirty years ago when I first found a set of Viking rune stones. Some time later I found Tarot cards based on Greek mythology figures and stories. I had developed an interest in ancient Greece from my college days and the book that accompanied the cards is a brilliant insight into the human condition.

Over the years I have added to my collection with spirit stones, I Ching and other cards and these all live in the black-velvet-lined wooden chest. I have dried lavender at the bottom and a handful of sheep's wool.

In 1996 I went back to England and while there visited some friends in Wales. I found the wool on a fence at their place overlooking the sea and brought it home with me. While in Wales, my friend took me out one day and we climbed a small mountain. The view all around was staggering but what affected me more was the tingle I felt through my whole being as we stood on the summit. It was an added connection to the earth that I am always aware of, especially when the traumas of life come to call.

Am I superstitious? Yes, without a doubt. Well, if that's what it means to be open to the signs that come our way. I'm not interested in the 'Madam Lola' draped in hippy clothes assuring me she can tell my future. I love to sit quietly and draw the cards for myself and read the definitions in the books that accompany them. I liken it to reading any book. Sometimes it can be reading something that jumped off the shelf and said 'take me home' but turns out to be so frustrating, yet I am unable to put it down and walk away. I know there is a hidden message and I keep reading till a group of words resonates inside and I get the feeling 'of course – that's what I'm reading this for'.

I suppose like everything, moderation is the key. I knew a woman a long time ago who had become dependent on what her Tarot cards told her and became incapable of making any decision without consulting them first. A time of quiet introspection helps us clear our thoughts and learn what is in our hearts, and this influences our decisions. I don't believe there is any requirement to ask the cards all the time; it is more important to trust in my instincts and faith that I will always have what is right for me when it is right.

I have noticed that like many people who live alone, I gave names to belongings. My bicycle – the one that was later stolen – was Beatrice and my car was Pegasus. We were mooching around a Sunday market and found the perfect rug for my studio. It's blue/grey and black to represent the ocean and has six dolphins leaping out of the water with their delightful smiles. As soon as we laid the rug down, I called the dolphins Dave, Dee, Dozy, Beaky, Mick and Titch. For those who have had a sheltered upbringing, this was the name of a pop group popular in England during the 1960s. I have no idea now what they sang that made them catch our attention then – perhaps it was the name of the group rather than the music.

I have a two-seater settee that converts to a bed. I have found if I lie on the settee during the day to read, I usually fall asleep. But on a couple of occasions we have had visitors who have slept on it as a bed and no one has complained.

A living creature

I have written about what is inside my studio, or my eyrie as we often call it. I am almost afraid to try and write about the view from my eyrie window. I have written any number of poems, little snapshots of the sighting of dolphins, a gull diving for lunch or a pelican flying past so close I feel I could almost touch it, but...

Our home sits close beside a tidal reach. I mean really close. The small garden, a strip of grass and a footpath are about twenty metres in width. And that's it. The morning after we moved in, we were astonished and alarmed to see that the river had come up over its banks and onto the path. We wondered if it would come into the garden and house but no, it turned out to have been a particularly high king tide; one of the jetties at the beach nearby had a whole section washed away.

The water is a living creature. I can think of no better way to describe it. Although it is referred to as the Port River, it is not fed by a meandering stream pouring down from the hills. It is a long inlet that snakes its way inland and ends a short distance south of where we live.

I am hopeless at estimating distances but I suppose the reach is two hundred metres across. On the far side directly opposite are rows of units in blocks of varying heights and designs. They give us an interesting skyline, especially in the evening when the sky has turned to apricot after the sun has set. We joke about how few lights appear in them at night and how few people are ever seen walking along that side of the reach, but this adds to the quiet atmosphere we are surrounded by.

There is a marina on that far side downstream from us and there are never more than two or three boats moored there. For a while, one of them was an old fishing boat. A young man lived on it with his dog and two white ducks. We think he was up to no good, as all identifying marks had been removed from the hull. He had an ingenious platform affair with a hole in the centre with an arrangement whereby he could lower lobster or crab pots on a windlass. He had a set-up that smacked of a small industry and I was quite impressed. But one day some neighbours spotted him and there were some colourful exchanges. He was reported to the Harbour and Fisheries Department and his boat was searched. All very dramatic. They obviously didn't find anything amiss but who really knows? One morning I looked out of the window as usual and the fishing boat had gone. A few weeks later it appeared downstream round by Dock One and later the boat was gone but the rig was still there. All very mysterious.

Also on the far side, set in a sort of corner where the railway line comes around the bend and crosses over the water on one of those old-fashioned steel girder bridges, is an area of mangroves. We have grown so used to the trains squeaking as they go around the bend that we hardly notice them. But when we sit out on the balcony and have our morning coffee or lunch we are full of scorn for the train drivers who slow right down when they go across the bridge. I've never been much interested in trains before, but now I find it amusing to identify the 'oners' and 'twoers' (indicating the number of carriages) and whether they are old or new. It is the kind of gentle silly game we play in this easy-going lifestyle.

But back to the mangrove corner. When the tide goes out, we can see the skeletons of two ships that foundered on the mud flats. This is a favourite place for the seagulls, sacred ibis, pelicans, cormorants, the grey and the white egrets. The hull of one of the ships was a clearly defined skeleton with its ribs reaching up like arms waiting to embrace someone, but strong tides, or perhaps one of the occasional violent storms, exerted enough power to break the back of the hull and it has flopped down like a tired ballerina. It's sad to see it like this and we wonder whether eventually it will all just get washed away. For a while one summer, it took on a flamboyant festive air. It was draped elegantly in vivid emerald green slime. That sounds ugly but it really was spectacular.

In front of the mud flats and about halfway across the reach is a row of old wooden posts. They are all that's left to show where timber was stored on the water awaiting its removal to the timber mills. Some quixotic person has allowed an art installation here. On five of the poles are life-size figures of people swimming in different actions – just the top part of their torso, arms and heads. They are quite striking.

The pelicans love to perch on top of the posts and it is usually where our eyes go to to check how high the water is. There are often up to half a dozen pelicans that grace us with their presence but there is a solitary one who is here most of the time. Even as I'm writing, I glanced up and he was drifting past my window as if checking up on me. Our eyes have met many times.

Some research has informed me the pelican is a symbol of buoyancy. Years ago I worked out no matter how far I went down emotionally or spiritually I would always come up again. Apparently the pelican is the symbol of this. How apt that is and how comforting when my tail feathers drag a bit with life in all its glory.

There have been many times when we have just stopped in our tracks to watch these amazing creatures in flight. They soar high on the thermals or skim just above the water raising themselves just a little with each beat of their wings to keep their wing tips dry. Then they rise and settle with infinite majesty to land on one of the posts.

The dolphins have become special friends. Right from the beginning there has been one that cruises on the surface quite close to the house. I felt it held the spirits of those I have loved who are no longer physically in my life. It has provided me with much comfort. There are dolphins out there almost every day and to watch them leaping and circling is like being with a newborn baby. They are delightful time-wasters – it's very hard to keep moving along with daily chores when they're providing us with such joyous displays.

Many times I've been called from sleep by the dolphins with their splashes and soft coughing sound. I love to go out onto the balcony and watch the ripples on the water. The orange and white reflected street lights on the opposite bank shiver and shake. Best of all is when there is a moon. To see moonlight shining off the wet sides of the dolphins is pure magic. The water becomes like a piece of dancing black velvet studded with moving shards of light.

How do I describe water? I'm an early morning person by nature and so every day when I get out of bed the first thing I do is look out to the reach. And more often than not – much to Stephen's amusement – I exclaim, 'It's still out there.' I don't mean it is still *there*, I mean it's so *still*. It looks more like a pond than a tidal reach. I wrote a poem about it, drawing a likeness to a not-quite-set jelly. Then after a few minutes it's as if a monster is on the riverbed and turning over. A very subtle shiver ripples over the surface. Any clouds and the units across the other side are perfectly reflected. It's early in the morning and in the evening when the reach has a certain quality and I believe it has something to do with the lack of direct sunlight. The world seems to pause just for a little while and it's wonderful to pause with it.

We have learned that it's unwise to use the direction of the wavelets to assess which way the tide is running. For ages I watched the tide 'coming in' and yet the water level shown by the posts was clearly going down. It's something to do with the wind but fun when we have guests to see their puzzlement so like our own.

As the sun turns towards the west in the afternoons, the river is transformed into a river of light. This brilliance is then reflected into the house and while the downside is that we do get hot in the summer, we are kept warmer in the winter. Just for a few moments in the summer evenings, the light shines through the upstairs and downstairs windows into the hallway and this normally shaded area comes alive. There is no sensible explanation, it just reminds me of… Well, I had to stop there and think…and think again because I don't think I can describe what that quality of light reminds me of. It's nothing like the dappled green light in the tree house. I suppose it's more like the sunlight blazing through enormous windows in a skyscraper. There is a hard clarity to it, but it's the clarity of life, like rainbows dancing in the hearts of diamonds. But it's also like being underwater with the mottled effect of moving lozenges of brightness.

We are most fortunate that we rarely get boats at this end of the reach. Having said that, there is something luxurious about the sound of oars creaking in the early morning. I am always reminded of images of the Thames with its dark green waters and skirts of willows and rowing eights skimming gracefully along its surface. Well, these rowboats skim the same but the waters are usually grey and blue. We get an assortment of kayaks and even an occasional tinnie puttering along taking hopeful fishermen to a secluded corner. The worst visitors have to be the jet skis. We were so incensed the first time a pair screamed into our Sunday afternoon serenity that I immediately rang the authorities. I was dejected to hear that legally the jet-skiers were allowed to be out there providing they kept to the speed limit of seven kilometres per hour. Now who was ever going to be able to clock their speed? Happily this insanity has only revisited us once and we can only hope the waters are too boring to make it worthwhile coming again.

Recently the Flotilla for Kids was held downstream from us. It's held each year to help raise funds for children with cancer and similar conditions. It was a wonderful sight seeing so many yachts and sailing craft coming up the river. Just for a while it was easy to imagine what it would have been like seventy years ago when the Port was a thriving place. We have a photograph dated 1948 of an aerial view of the tidal reach and there are tall ships moored directly in front of where our house now stands. How it must have hummed with activity.

There are many things in this area that are worthy of comment, but I'd like to single out another art installation. There is a small area of grass just along the reach from our house and there stand five life-size emus – one even has a clutch of eggs between its feet. But what really makes them noteworthy is their colour. They are fluorescent green – well, they were when first put there. Fortunately they have become faded and a bit weathered. Adults and children alike seem to be drawn to them. What not many people know is that they glow in the dark. I have fun imagining the reaction of a drunk as he walks along the path. I don't think he would want to come this way again and who would believe him if he tried to tell anyone?

But for us, we are just so pleased that the reach is like a place separated from the rest of the world by a bend in the river.

Visitors or companions

It seems another interest Stephen and I share is having birds in the garden. For many years I have left bread crumbs and birdseed out and enjoyed the pleasure of watching the different birds. The tree house was surrounded by enormous gum trees and so parrots flocked there. I loved to watch the rosellas hang upside-down on the washing line to eat the seed in the hanging dish. The magpies would sit on the balcony railing and sing and chortle till I came out and fed them early in the morning. They even brought their babies down and while they were funny to watch I felt so sorry for the parent birds as a baby almost their own size squawked even as they were putting food into its mouth.

Stephen had enjoyed parrots in his garden in Canberra so it wasn't surprising we both hoped we could encourage parrots into this one. Well, it hasn't happened yet. Oh, they zoom over the garden screeching messages to each other, and occasionally stop for a drink from the bird bath on the river side, but they don't stop and investigate the birdseed. We see and hear a lot of them as we walk to the local shops and are enchanted by their brilliant plumage.

When we first moved in to the river house, a turtle dove managed to come indoors. We carefully took it back out in the garden, but we must have done something right as she stays close by. We have watched in fascination as she built a nest in the lilly pilly tree by the front door only to see her dismantle it before it was complete and start another. We affectionately called her Dopey Dora. She liked to hop onto one of the solar garden lights and then onto the feeding stand. Before too long, Dora was joined by another dove and that was when things began to get confusing. It looked as if we had it wrong and Dora was really Dorian. Dorian is very amorous, or would like to be, and almost daily is seen strutting his stuff trying to seduce Dora on top of the garage roof. He has occasionally succeeded but mostly she gets impatient with him and flies off. When the landlord cut the lilly pilly tree down, we wondered where Dora went to build her nests, but there is no point in asking her. Dora or Dorian can still surprise, us. The latest antic was to get inside the container we keep the birdseed in. Stephen's little grandson decided to put birdseed into the birdbath and left the lid off the container. I suppose there was some bird logic in Dora or Dorian falling in!

Not so nice are the crested pigeons. They are bullies and cowards. They sit up on the garage roof watching us have our breakfast and waiting till we go indoors before they come down. They manage to push everyone else aside and usually, in their clumsiness, knock the seed-holder down onto the ground. From a distance they are quite striking with the topknot that gives them an almost eagle-like profile. But we don't like their red eyes. There's no hint of the gentleness of the turtle doves. We call them hoodlums or even the Gestapo when they are particularly aggressive.

What garden doesn't have sparrows? There are up to thirty in the flock that frequent our garden. They sit on next door's washing line or the dividing fence and send down two or three to reconnoitre the garden. Gradually they all come down to feast. They are always so cheerful and friendly. At other times they seem to congregate in the bushes that beyond all reason cling to the river bank. When I cycle along the path I'm always surprised, as the bushes don't appear to be giving refuge to anything; then suddenly a dozen or so sparrows take flight from its foliage.

The New Holland honeyeaters are exactly like the ones I had at the tree house. They delight in taking turns playing in the bird bath. They squabble and screech to each other like a pack of schoolchildren. They are timid, though, and at any quick movement they fly away.

Stephen has a running altercation with blackbirds. I love to hear their song in the early morning and late evening. There is something majestic about their unrelieved black plumage and the vivid gold beak. So why do they upset Stephen? Well, he's a man who likes our garden to look tidy, with well-swept pathways. We've put bark chips on the flower beds either side of the path to the front door. And that is where the trouble is. The blackbirds scuff and scratch the bark aside to get to the little bugs hiding underneath. Mostly the bark ends up on the path. And that does not make Stephen a happy chappy.

I used to like to watch the starlings in the garden too, till there was a rather unfortunate incident. For most of the day, a baby starling could be seen in the garden. It kept trying to fly up onto and over the garden fence. It wouldn't have anything to eat and I was worried about its chances of survival. Then a parent bird came down and fed it some breadcrumbs and that set my mind at rest – a bit. I was concerned that the little bird wouldn't survive the night, as a neighbour's cat likes to sleep under our bushes. With some reluctance, I went out into the garden the next morning. When there was no sign of the bird, I thought it must have managed to get over the fence and flown away. Later I looked over the edge of the upstairs balcony and sure enough the little bird had made it over the fence, but it had come to a sticky end by being run over by a passing vehicle. I'm right off starlings at the moment despite their beautiful glossy plumage that reminds me of oil on a puddle in the road. I think the parent birds have got the message, because they have been missing for quite a while now.

Most days, we have our lunch on the upstairs balcony overlooking the reach. The seagulls appear to watch us from the mudflats on the far side. If one of us stands up or waves an arm, a flock of the gulls come racing over to see what we've thrown them for lunch. They huddle on the grass outside the garden abusing each other. Some will fly overhead and even land on the railing. Like most people, I expect, we try to see if there is an injured one we can feed our crusts to. It seems a little odd to us that they don't at all like coming down into the garden. Whether it has something to do with the fences we don't know. They really are beautiful in their own way and brilliant in flight. Some have that cold calculating look that the crested pigeons have, though, and can be nasty to the other gulls.

Last winter for weeks, our sleep was disturbed by something scrabbling about on the roof. For a short time after we first moved in, a black rabbit made its home in the garden. It was quite tame and looked very picturesque sitting on the lawn eating clover. Then it just wasn't there any more. Well, obviously it wasn't the rabbit on the roof but was it the rabbit that was eating the plants? I had made a small vegetable garden and was dismayed to come out the following morning to find the snow peas had been nibbled to nothing. The same with the carrot tops. A more careful check of the garden over a period of time showed that whenever a plant sent out new growth, it disappeared overnight. Roses, native violets, some of the herbs on the herb table, all were munched. In desperation I bought some nylon netting and made little circus tents over all the plants that were getting eaten. It seemed to work and everything flourished, even if the garden did look a little odd. Then we noticed that the scrabbling on the roof stopped, so it looked like the midnight muncher had given up and gone to raid someone else's garden. The garden is looking especially lovely these days but every morning I go out with some trepidation in case our visitor has returned – I certainly would if I was it and knew how well everything was doing.

I find visiting birds give me a lovely sense of affirmation that we really are kind and gentle people. On two occasions we have been blessed for a few brief moments with unexpected visitors. We came home from the shops and sitting on our chairs by the table under the veranda were a pair of white doves. They must have been pets they were so tame. Then, as suddenly as they came, they were gone. Another time, I glanced out of the window to the garden on the reach side and there was a brilliant yellow bird. At first I thought it might have been a canary but careful consultation with the bird book showed it was a finch. Like the doves, it only stayed a short while but we took some photographs and have lovely memories.

When we first moved in, one of my sons warned me against putting bread crumbs down on the lawns. He been sitting on the rocks beside the water and a rat had come out to see what he was up to. Sometimes when we're sitting on the balcony having lunch we see a rat running between the shelter of the rocks and the community litter bin. We call it Ratty, as if from *Wind in the Willows*, and it was that thought that inspired me to write about our life beside the river. One morning while cycling along the path, I noticed a V shape ahead of me in the still water. I was intrigued, as it looked just like an otter. When I could get close enough to identify it, it turned out to be our rat friend or one of his relatives. They are incredibly graceful in the water and for a few moments it was good to forget all the horrible stories that are told about rats.

Simple routines

Stephen and I are creatures of habit and we thrive on the simple routines that shape our daily lives. Throughout spring and summer and into autumn, we breakfast under the veranda. We watch the birds as they contemplate coming down to feed. We utter our displeasure at the hooligan topknot pigeons. But mostly we soak up the gentle peace of the garden and the early morning sunshine.

After I have washed the dishes and made the bed, every weekday we walk down to the local post office to empty the mail box. I'm always excited when we find a blue, red or yellow card in the box as this indicates there is a package to be collected from inside. And packages to Stephen are manuscripts. Someone has slaved for countless hours, pouring out thoughts onto numerous pages, and sent their work into the press in the hope of a dream coming true – becoming a published author. We don't just hold an envelope in our hands; we are holding hopes, dreams and aspirations. This is part of my new life I am so thrilled by: sitting in the cosy corner reading a new manuscript. It wasn't easy at first, but I am learning how to detach myself enough to be able to say, 'This has something' or 'I love this', or the other side, 'There are a lot of words but they aren't saying anything.' Stephen always has the final say and I certainly don't envy him the task of returning a manuscript with a polite rejection slip.

At a recent book launch I struck up a conversation with a woman I had never met before. Then she made herself known to me and I was so pleased I could say, 'I've read your manuscript three times preparing it for print. It was a wonderful read.' I could even quote a piece that had resonated deeply with me. She then went on to tell me how some of it was based on things that really happened in her family long ago.

I hope it isn't vanity but I do read all the books we launch. It's important to me when I'm hoping to sell copies that I can talk at least a little about the contents. I've learned that I might not always like the subject matter but if the writer has a light touch or an unusual perspective, I love to bring this to the attention of prospective buyers because, when all is said and done, the writers want their 'babies' to be read.

Collecting packages frequently at the post office has enabled us to build up a delightful rapport with the ladies in there. When Stephen had a run-in with cancer, these ladies could not have been more supportive. It started out as a bit of a joke. Stephen was to be in hospital for almost two weeks, which meant I had to empty the box. And our mail box is on the top row and, even standing on the step, I can't reach deeply into it. So I asked when they sorted the mail could they please make sure it was pushed to the front. From that moment, they have been watching us with a maternal eye and to our delight accepted the invitation to come to our last book launch.

Stephen cooks the evening meal in our house and prefers to shop every day. This has been quite a change for me who hates shops and used to shop once a week. We have a favourite woman we go to at the check-out and she comments if we go in later during the day or if we don't go in at all. We call her 'our lady of the blessed check-out', but not to her face. This reminds me of the days of village shops or the corner deli where the shopkeepers knew most of their customers and their habits and kept an eye on people. Port Adelaide has been a working port for many years and has had a reputation for roughness. No one can deny this. But these days it is very quiet and our local shopping centre has become more like a small country town of long ago.

We walk home along the path beside the canal and check out the height of the water, what pelicans and other birds are about, and we are always on the alert for dolphins. But we watch other things too. The back gardens of a row of houses face the canal. One garden has a very large trampoline which seems to provide a comfortable resting place for an equally large Great Dane. This dog is beautiful and sometimes manages a deep throaty woof as we walk past. Another garden is interesting because it's obviously looked after by a keen gardener. They have wonderfully tall sunflowers that they put plastic bags over – presumably to catch the seeds, or stop the parrots eating them. During winter they have a spectacular show of sweet peas climbing the fence. Oh, how I envy them this.

We watched in horror and disgust as a new house was built. It comes out into the block much further than the next-door neighbour's and effectively blocks their view of the reach and the corner where the mudflats are. The wall overlooking the canal has been cemented over and painted cream, which isn't too bad, but there is a hideous side wall that is just natural and very unpleasant brick. Bad enough to have spoiled the view but to do this as well smacks of a total lack of consideration for their neighbours.

One of my favourite people we look out for is a small woman, quite elderly, who is bent over and needs a walking stick to help her get about. But we often see her walking her dogs and she is always cheerful. We get concerned if we don't see her for a few days.

One time we had Stephen's then four-year-old granddaughter with us. She is a true Virgo. She always spots litter and demands to know who left it there and why. Her outrage knew no bounds when a shopping trolley was left on the path near the park. Now every time we see a stray trolley Stephen pipes up, mimicking the child exactly with 'Who left that there?' Sometimes he even tacks on a 'That's naudy.' Little girls can be so earnest.

We don't just walk, we progress along the pathway. We watch plants and flowers blossom, commenting on the colours. We speculate on when the council will mow the grass in the park. We stop and admire parrots. We count the empty units and wonder when someone will move in. Always we look in the reach in the hope of seeing the shoals of fish that seem to stay close to the rocky banks. Not so nice are the jellyfish that appear in the summer.

After our excursion to the post office, we have morning coffee either in the garden or upstairs on the balcony. During the summer we notice that by 10.30 the sun is really hot so, more often than not, we go upstairs to the balcony overlooking the reach.

Lunch has always been upstairs. When we first moved in, one Saturday morning we were enjoying prawns, brown bread and sparkling wine. I threw my bread crusts over the railing with the idea the birds would eventually find them on the garden below. A few people just happened to be walking along the river path as I did this and of course Stephen quipped about me feeding prawn tails to the peasants. Another of those precious connections.

It has been a mystery to us why there are so few people to be seen on the other side of the reach. This means that while we sit on the balcony we find ourselves commenting on anyone who does appear. Such excitement one day when we spotted people having lunch on one of the balconies and even more people standing on another balcony watching the dolphins.

My curiosity had been aroused and one morning when I went out for my bike ride before breakfast I deliberately cruised along the path on that side of the reach. I suspect the sun is the reason people don't gather much over there. It glares so hard and bright off the water that it's impossible to see anything. I could hear splashing and could see the far-reaching ripples, which meant either dolphins or cormorants were active in the water, but could see nothing.

After lunch is when we go out into the world again for things like banking and posting packages of books to customers. We see different people on this trip. Our local greengrocer goes by the name of Farmer Joe. Stephen has a remarkable command of the English language and one of the things I love so much about him is his willingness to have fun with language. I have to say this keeps me on my mental toes. It's all about punctuation, really. I innocently said, 'Are we going to Farmer Joe's later?' Stephen's immediate response was something like 'Oh, is he Farmer Joe Slater now?' and of course this name has stuck. I'm not sure if that translates into an amusing anecdote; suffice it to say he does little things like this to me all the time and I'm often hard pressed to work out what I said and how he has tweaked it.

Our afternoons seem to drift by. Stephen in his office downstairs doing what he calls 'unremitting toil'. As if. He loves words, he loves editing and publishing. As he said once, he's lucky enough to have a hobby he can make just enough money out of to make a living. I'm not sure if he really grasps the enormity of the change he can make to a person's life by publishing their 'baby'. Well, not until he met me anyway. He knows he has turned my life completely inside out and upside down. It was a wonderful accolade when he was making a speech at a function and acknowledged it was disconcerting being included in a writer's poems. Suddenly he is not as removed as he was, but I think he enjoys this new view.

My afternoons are spent in my studio preparing manuscripts for printing, or reading, writing or painting. My eyes are constantly taking in life on the reach. When it is hot, I reluctantly have to draw the curtains. I hate having to shut myself in – or is it the view out? I remember all those years I worked for the Public Service. I loved my job but my only complaint was that I had to sit in an office to do it. I pleaded for a long extension cord so I could sit in the park but this was refused. Now I face the outside world and I couldn't want for more. In the late afternoon, the sun reflects off the water and turns it into literally a river of light. It glares so much I have to make a decision to either stop work or shut the curtains. But what choices I have. I am sooo lucky.

We both stop about 4 p.m. and meet in the cosy corner and usually read or do word puzzles. When I was a child, I loved to hear my mother pottering about the kitchen making the evening meal. Now I have this again as Stephen prepares our dinner. It's my task to lay the table. We each have our favourite place, which means we can both look out onto the water while we eat. It's also my task to make dessert, which is usually fresh fruit. So hard to prepare! I wash the dishes, which is no hardship. Then we settle down and watch old movies.

Our days are not always this quiet. We like to go into Adelaide now and then. It is such a hoot travelling on the train for free now we have our Seniors Cards. We usually end up going into the book shop in the mall that is the single one remaining out of the three or four we used to be able to choose from. When you have a writer and a publisher together, it's guaranteed one of us will buy at least one book. I find I prefer second-hand book shops these days.

Stephen knows I love to get a 'tree fix' in the Botanic Gardens. I never tire of wandering around among the trees and flower beds. Adelaide is extremely fortunate to have two Botanic Gardens. Mount Lofty overlooks the city and the coastal plain for many miles. But unknown to many, on the far side of the mountain are the gardens. There is a small lake right at the bottom, but to get there are lots of little winding paths. My favourite takes me through an area called the Woodland Glade. A small touch of England. There is a link between both of these gardens and libraries, and, I suppose, old churches too. A reverence. Something in the atmosphere that makes us talk in hushed whispers, if at all. A few times we have wandered through the gardens in the city: it's like stepping into another world and we have enjoyed a Devonshire tea at the little kiosk.

Other times when we visit the city we'll go to the Central Market and have a cheap Asian meal for lunch. In the market we indulge ourselves with purchasing delicious cold meats, cheeses and different breads. Having a grazing meal is such a treat.

Stephen has taught me the fun to be had in places like Bunnings, Officeworks, CD shops, Reject Shops and Ikea. I'm still not very good at browsing but I am improving. But then Stephen has taught me to appreciate a lot of things differently.

Looking in the window

For far too many years, I felt I was standing out in the cold, looking in the window of other people's lives with a deep sense of longing. While creating my fictitious dream house on paper, I knew it wasn't just a pile of bricks I wanted.

Recently we launched my latest book of poetry and the wonderful feeling of warmth and goodwill was extended beyond the event in the bookshop. That same evening we had four friends round for a celebratory meal.

There was a moment or two when I imagined I was outside on the path by the reach. We had left the curtains undrawn as it was a mild evening and some of our friends still hadn't seen dolphins even though they have visited several times. There was always the chance the dolphins would swim past and splash the water to call us out to admire them.

What I saw in my mind's eye was a large room softly lit. Bookcases lined one wall, pot plants and vases of flowers rested randomly; the cosy corner looked so inviting with its soft cushions and small table laden with books.

Six people stood around avidly talking about the afternoon's events. Stephen put the finishing touches to dinner and those six people moved to sit around the dining table. Wine glasses raised in a toast sparked with light. Plain white dishes were being passed from one person to the next as they helped themselves to generous portions of rabbit and vegetables. There was the rise and fall of voices, a sudden burst of laughter.

This wasn't just two like-minded people. All six of us had in common the love of words. Between us we were or had at some time been teacher, journalist, librarian, publisher, owners of a book shop and political activist, and four of us were published poets. None of us were overly concerned with material wealth.

With Stephen's run-in with cancer not far distant in time, we were all keenly aware of the fragility of life and the importance of making the most of every day. Even now, sharing a simple meal cannot be taken for granted. But I think Epicurus would be proud of us if it were he standing outside the window.

Good food, good wine, good company and good conversation. It doesn't come much better than this.

It's Still Out There

Introduction

In 2010, Stephen was diagnosed with a cancer in his gum that resulted in drastic surgery, a couple of weeks in hospital and six eternal weeks of radiotherapy. When all that was done and we were left to recover, I wrote *Down by the River*. It was my way of reminding myself of all the small details that make up this wonderful life I have with Stephen. Writing it down was my way of making it real.

The giant and unrelenting medical system kept us in its grip and every three months we trotted off to the hospital for Stephen's check-up and we sighed with relief as each time he was given a clean bill of health. I felt like we were being given some sort of tick of approval for being good and could be granted some more time. And we are indeed fortunate. After the most recent appointment, and all continuing to be well, these trips will be yearly.

But we were forever changed by this rude intrusion.

All my adult life I have been aware of the need to make each day count. I have never been very good at making long-term plans and trying to second-guess what the future might hold in store for me and those I love. But if I have made someone feel good about themselves, or I have brought a smile to someone's face, perhaps by sharing a wonder of nature I have witnessed, then the days do count. The rightness of this general philosophy has been reinforced several times over the years, usually when something awful and unexpected occurs.

Yesterday the sound of birdsong woke me up. I half-opened one eye and saw it was almost six o'clock. I slipped out of bed and padded silently into the guest bedroom. I went to the window and noted that Venus was brilliantly shining straight at me. I smiled and whispered, 'Good morning.' There were a few smudges of cloud over the hills so I knew that there would soon be a pretty sunrise. But I was unsettled.

I had been reading *Eat Pray Love* by Elizabeth Gilbert and her search for herself in her relationship with her god, and how meditation was a key part of her ongoing awareness. It had contributed to my feeling of being unsettled, because my routine of years had been interrupted and I hadn't been meditating at the start of my days. And without that silent centring, my thoughts fly all over the place and old insecurities try and sneak in.

After breakfast I went out for my usual bike ride to the beach and as I plodded along the waterline I made two decisions. I returned home with a sense of purpose that had been missing for months.

There are words of wisdom I became aware of years ago and I often misquote them. Their essence is that all things change in order to stay the same. So once again I find myself poised in front of the computer, looking out across the mirror-like tidal reach, watching the night sky gradually disappear into the west, and soft pink clouds heralding a new day and think, 'It's still out there.' I do need to write it down to make it real.

That was yesterday's first decision. The other decision? To dig up the broad beans of course.

The scent of broad beans

For years, my mother has talked of writing her memoirs of life in a tiny English village; The Scent of Broad Beans was to be the title. I think perhaps it brought back memories of the struggles of a young town-raised woman, thrust by war into the Land Army, where she met my dad. Sometimes I think that the certificate she won for her ability to plough a straight furrow was one of her most prized possessions. After the war ended, they married and moved into a tied cottage, then quickly had three children, and life for them was set. My dad was an agricultural mechanic and he farmed for someone else. I heard he hungered to come to Australia but as far as I know he hardly went out of the county he was born and died in. He died over thirty years ago but he is a constant in my life – especially when I am pottering in our vegetable garden.

Vegetable garden sounds rather grand and probably conjures up images of long, straight rows of potatoes, peas, beans, carrots and cabbages. Our vegetable patch is literally that – a patch. Probably about the same size as our dining table. When we first moved in to the river house, a lilly pilly stood close to the front door. It provided great shade for Stephen's office and shelter for the birds, but the owner wasn't impressed by the way it leaned on the guttering, filling it with leaves, and he cut it down. Suddenly we had this space and I decided it would be ideal to grow vegetables in.

I have grown carrots, beetroot and spring onions, but the tomatoes and cucumbers have been the best crops till now. Months ago I decided to grow broad beans and when the tomatoes were finished at the end of the summer I duly dug lots of organic fertiliser into the ground and planted the twenty or so seeds that were all the garden would hold.

Every day we sit under the veranda in front of Stephen's office and have morning coffee. Our little table is right beside the vegetable patch so I have watched as the first shoots appeared. I worried when some didn't come up and Stephen's then seven-year-old granddaughter, Ella, was enchanted with the idea they had gone to China. But it never does to be impatient with Mother Nature and in time all the beans came up.

I had chosen the seeds carefully, finding something new to me: dwarf broad beans. I thought this would be a good idea as if beans grow too tall there can be problems with the wind blowing them down and breaking the stems. The trouble was, the beans themselves hadn't read the packet and as winter wore on the beans grew taller and taller. Some ended up well over my head. (Thank you, but no comments about my lack of height, please. Being five feet one inch tall is quite enough for me.)

Masses of flowers appeared, along with lots of bees, and lo and behold, in time, I had little broad bean pods growing. As you can probably tell, it was the smell of the flowers that brought back all those memories of my own growing up on the farm. My mother was delighted when I told her about them and off she went on a little riff about the book she will never write now because she has lost her sight. She also gave me a little lecture about looking for blackfly, which are the scourge of growing broad beans in England. Well, mine didn't ever get blackfly, but I did wonder when I saw a line of ants walking along the support strings. Oh yes, the beans grew so tall I had to prop them up with a system of stakes and strings. Stephen has a quixotic sense of humour and the schoolboy that was re-released by the long hours under anaesthetic during his surgery found wicked pleasure in flicking the strings so the tightrope-walking ants fell off and had to start again.

The first lot of beans were ready for picking and I admit I stepped into another world as I filled the bucket with fat pods. Was I looking for a sense of continuity? Possibly. It was near my sixty-third birthday and I came to Australia on my twenty-first. I'll save you doing the arithmetic: I have been in this country for more than two-thirds of my life. I have been heard to say many, many times that I have no regrets coming here to live – but I do have my sorrows. Among these, naturally, is not seeing much of my family, who continue to live in England. My thoughts drifted to my trip to England in 1985 and staying briefly with my brother Steve. He was growing broad beans just like our dad had done for years. He had lovely straight rows too; typical of him to be so methodical. He would have a good laugh to see my little patch, but not unkind laughter, I think.

Stephen made an incredible dip with our first lot of beans. He loves cooking and he does this a bit like Steve does things – methodically. He chooses his recipes with care and follows the instructions. His reasoning, echoing our friend Ken, is that if he likes it, he can make it the same another time. Stephen had seen me sitting under the veranda shucking the beans, absent-mindedly eating the little ones raw. He knew I had travelled back in time to the farmhouse when shucking beans and peas was part of the Sunday lunch ritual.

A while later when I wandered into the kitchen, I was assailed by the smell of the beans cooking. Hmm. Then to bring me right back to today and this life, the smell of toasting cumin seeds filled the air. These ended up with the mashed-up beans. We sat out on the balcony at lunchtime and had Turkish bread, broad bean dip and glasses of sparkling wine. How decadent is that!

One day when we were looking after Ella, she helped me pick some beans and we sat together at the little round table to shuck them. She is very much a nature child and it warmed my heart to hear her say quite spontaneously, 'This is fun,' as we scrabbled among the towering bean plants. We gave her a garden kit when she was younger, as she was longing to grow things. She soon learned that plants need constant attention during the hot summer days and I think a lot of the glamour evaporated like the water she poured on her herbs and flowers. I noticed she didn't mention growing plants of her own. I am just glad she enjoyed helping me harvest our crop.

The decision to dig up the bean plants was made because Ella and I had picked just about all of the beans and there were only a few flowers right at the top of the plants but they were getting so tall and even with assistance were falling about all over the place. So when I arrived home from my bike ride, I dug up the beans, getting just enough for one last batch to have with dinner. My thoughts are already drifting towards tomatoes and cucumbers for the summer.

Some things will never be the same again

While Stephen was in hospital, our friend Ray visited and quietly named him the Stoic. He was absolutely right. Stephen was determined to get home as quickly as possible and to that end was the model, so-called compliant, patient. He did everything that was asked of him, never complained and everyone could see how hard he worked to be able to regain his independence. However, the real evidence of that stoicism was revealed over the subsequent two years or so.

None of us understood the far-reaching effects of the surgery or the radiotherapy. The blessing of being in shock protected us at first. I won't say we grew accustomed to anything as the shock wore off, because we didn't. We do talk about things a little at a time, and that is where I am reminded Stephen has to live with these restrictions every moment of every day, whereas I can forget them for long periods. And, right or wrong, I do.

Part of the surgical procedure was to remove a piece of Stephen's jawbone and replace it with a piece of bone taken from his hip. Apart from people recoiling and nervously laughing when he offers to show them the scar across his hip, which is probably twelve inches long, I think we all forget about this. He had to learn how to walk again in the hospital and I thought he would need a walking stick for ages, but no, as soon as he got home, he climbed up the stairs to prove he could and refused to use the cane again. Only now has he conceded how painful that action was. I have no idea for how long walking was still painful. Since then we have climbed mountains in Tasmania, Mount Lofty here in Adelaide, Mount Gambier in the south-east and a big hill in Burra in the mid-north, so I guess it is safe to say his hip works. It's just our knees that complain these days.

Anyone who has had extensive dental work knows how disrupting to ordinary life it is. Even the little things like drinking a cuppa without spillage. Although we were told it would happen, I don't think either of us really appreciated that the quarter of Stephen's face that was operated on would be forever numb, like when you have injections at the dentist. Some of the nerves have re-wired themselves but the doctors admitted they could not predict what would heal and what wouldn't. They said it could take a couple of years to settle down but even that was only an educated guess.

Another part of the surgery entailed a chunk of his tongue being removed and this left limits to mobility and dexterity. It meant that not only has he had to deal with a mouth feeling like it was full of clouds, he had to learn how to eat again. One of his worst fears was not being able to control food on that side of his mouth and the resulting dribbling. It rarely happens now. This and learning how to open his mouth wider, though never again as wide as before, was a heart-breaking process to watch. I am so thankful his smile is now almost the same as it was in appearance. It has never stopped lighting up his face.

The radiotherapy left another legacy, possibly the worst. It damaged forever his taste buds and left his tongue with a permanent tingle that Stephen describes as being like when we have a forkful of food that has not been allowed to cool properly. Some months after the radiotherapy finished, we went to Tasmania. It was while staying with our friends Steve and Sue that he made a wonderful discovery. He could really taste the Tasmanian Riesling served with dinner. The joy of this was the best to witness. We had all been cast in the helpless chair and I think it made them feel really good that this discovery was made in their home at their dining table, especially as they had gone to so much trouble to provide a meal that would be easy for Stephen to eat.

Stephen loves a good curry. He still makes them, but admits he experiences tingles on top of the resident tingle. I can't begin to imagine what that sensation is like. I think the simple pleasure of eating has gone forever for Stephen. Sometimes I know something has hit the spot and he has enjoyed it, but the reality is, it doesn't happen very often. A meal in an Asian restaurant revealed the pleasure of eating duck! His love of mangoes is unchanged, possibly it has even increased. I suppose it is anything that is easy to eat but that is being dismissive. No one knows how much of the taste he is really getting.

Stephen has always been quietly spoken, but I notice lately that his voice is even softer. Either that or I am losing my hearing. Well, it could always be a combination of both, but it has opened up another area of frustration. Often I am now the voice. When we go to the hospital, the doctors direct their questions at Stephen and look to me for information. At other times when we are in conversations I have to make a conscious effort not to step in. Stephen still has a very powerful voice in what he has to say. He just says it quieter now.

Stephen loves to tease me and how can I resist his smile? I always end up laughing too. But there is something that hurts when he says, 'You'd like to smack me, wouldn't you? Here, this side.' It is the side that has a metal plate keeping his jaw together. There is a perfectly straight line across this cheek where the radiotherapy stopped. The redness has faded below this line, but his beard will never grow there again. Oh, and that area is colder to touch. The lines that have appeared on his face tell their own story.

Yet through all of this, Stephen has remained – stoic and cheerful. It seems to be one of those quirks of the human condition that the one most profoundly affected must be the one who teaches those around them. My mother says this often about being blind and she wearies of forever having to remind people of her restrictions and make allowances for their forgetfulness. I did it when my son died. Trying to make other people feel better because they were embarrassed or deeply moved when I said he took his own life. So Stephen has made us all feel more at ease with everything. As he says, 'No point in complaining.' So typical.

The right time, the right place

Living here down by the tidal reach with Stephen, and retiring from the strictures of office hours, I have at last been able to lay down so much grief and anger. The dolphins have played a very important part in this. How can I watch them arrowing through the water just below the surface, or leaping high and clear in sheer exuberance, and not be filled with wonder and joy?

In the past if I was feeling really unbalanced for some reason, I plumped down on the side of sadness. This felt safe. And, as they say, misery likes its own company and people left me alone when I was down. But Stephen with his calm approach to life has taught me there is a better way. He sees me getting bogged down in 'what-if…' and a million self-doubts, asks if I can change anything and, if not, well, stop it. So simple. Gradually when I felt this wavering, I found I was starting to smile to myself and was learning slowly but surely that life really is all good. Not just an ideal to be hungered for, but a reality that could withstand the harrowing fears and doubts that came with Stephen's run-in with cancer and being a parent and grandparent.

Very early in our relationship, Stephen gave me a ring to wear. An unusual design in white and yellow gold. We had the briefest of talks about getting married and both agreed we had both been married before and didn't feel the need to do that again.

2012 being a leap year, February had twenty-nine days and there is a legend that on this day, a girl can ask the man of her dreams to marry her, rather than waiting for him to ask her – or not. Over breakfast on the day, I mentioned to Stephen the legend and that I could ask him to marry me, and that was the end of that particular conversation. We carried on with our day as if nothing different had been said.

Over dinner that evening, Stephen wanted to know if I was going to ask him, or did he have to wait another four years. So this was it. One of those defining moments when a whole bunch of unexpected thoughts and feelings came crashing in and I realised I really wanted this. So I asked him to marry me and he said yes.

Just in case you are creating all kinds of romantic, intimate scenarios that went with this proposal, it must be said that there were three of us at the table that evening. Stephen has another granddaughter, Tizanne, aged nineteen, who lives in England with her mum Karyn and younger brother Joby. While she studied for a place at university, Tiz had worked at three jobs so she would have enough money to have a gap year in Australia. Hers is an extraordinary tale that I hope she will write down one day. After spending a couple of months along the east coast of Australia, she came to us halfway through December 2011 so she could have a family Christmas.

In between trips to Perth, Tasmania and Fiji and three months WWOOFFing and coaching in a gym, Tiz used our guest bedroom as her home base. (If, like us, you have never heard of WWOOFFing, it is worth looking up on Google. Essentially, travellers can work on officially listed organic farms in return for board and lodgings. It's a great way to see the country and save on living expenses. By doing eighty-eight days of it in her year here, Tiz earned an extra year on her work visa, which she can take advantage of any time until she is thirty-one.)

Tiz was a marvellous house guest. She fitted in with our lives with such ease and getting into the spirit of the way we live. I loved to listen to her and Stephen bantering. A very special relationship for certain. But this arrangement was also the reason my meditation routine took a dive.

Since retiring nearly three years ago, I have been going into the guest bedroom pretty much every morning to watch the dawn, and that is when I meditated. Even when Tiz was away, the room was hers and I didn't feel comfortable going in there. I was waiting for her to return to England before re-commencing my dawn watching, but that also felt strange because I wasn't in a hurry to see her go. It was complicated.

Having proposed and been accepted, nothing further happened. Telling our respective families was something we both had to do and we found we were reluctant. We both knew we had been accepted as partners but marriage was something else again.

The opportunity to tell Stephen's son Chris presented itself and after his initial surprise and some prompting from me that his blessing was very important to us, he embraced the whole idea. It was already in place that Karyn and Joby would be coming to Australia for a few weeks' holiday in July/August so it was an easy decision to have the celebration while they were here. Karyn loves cooking and organising so I was more than happy to hand over the task of setting up a smorgasbord of delicious things to eat and make our quiet home look festive. If I use her enthusiasm as a guide, then there could be no doubt we had her approval.

That left me to tell my sons, Alex, Noel and David. David and Amy were getting married in April. A beautiful wedding in the gardens of a winery. Amy is tall and regal and was just like a lily in a field of brightly coloured wild flowers – even when she shed her high heels and was walking around in thongs at the reception. The speeches were from the heart and tears were falling amongst the laughter. As always when my sons get together, I learned more about their growing up, a somewhat nerve-racking experience. I have great love and admiration for these boys, now men with heavy responsibilities, but always my babies. It warmed my heart that all three of them walked Stephen and me out to our car when we left.

Noel quipped, 'Well, that's the last wedding in the family till the kids grow up.'

I hesitated and blurted out, 'Well, that's not quite true.' I told them about the proposal and our plan to be married in August – date and so on to be fixed.

Their pleasure was indescribable. They are all big, tall men and they almost swamped Stephen in their response. Thanking him for making their mother smile and so happy.

We had the same positive reaction from everyone we told; well, not always the effusive hugs, but the delight was the same. I think people are essentially romantic and relish a love story. We often read about tears of joy, but how do I explain how it feels knowing Stephen and I prompted such a reaction? There was – is – a rightness to us getting married and there is no more to be said.

For myself I hadn't realised how old-fashioned I am. I had been fighting and rebelling for so many years, swearing I would never, ever settle *for* in a relationship. Somewhere in the turmoil of emotions, I found

I wasn't settling *for*, but I was settling *down* in the best possible way. I have stopped fighting for a place in the world, a place where I truly belong. Stephen and I love each other, we love our life together. We agreed we wanted to make this public statement of commitment to each other, our families and friends and the world we live in.

The when was easy. Where? No hesitation: it had to be here in our river house beside the tidal reach. The celebrant was also easy to choose. The Internet is a remarkable thing really and I quickly found a local celebrant who had the same family name as my mother before she married my dad. Serendipity? Why not? And she was absolutely the right person.

Our quiet home was buzzing and we wouldn't have thought it could have increased. Until Karyn's partner, Carl, who was waiting for her back in England, sent her a large bouquet of exquisite red roses and proposed. I'm not certain who was the most surprised when she accepted. It was lovely to see her so excited and happy about her future.

Our invitations went out bearing a picture of a pair of ducks. Stephen and I became the two old ducks getting married, a theme which quite a few of our guests picked up on – 'Um – hope you have a quacking good time,' from someone who couldn't make it.

Alex and Chris agreed to be witnesses. Noel was providing and cooking the barbecue. David and Noel's son Jamie were playing their guitars by the door to welcome guests. Peter was our master of ceremonies (and with our very fluid plans he did an amazing job), Joan provided me with red and white roses bound together with ribbon to symbolise unity, Ann wrote us a stunning poem, Ken and Rachel provided an old horseshoe for luck.

Helen, who is from Scotland, made the most brilliant shortbreads. Annette made Anzac biscuits, which she does so well. Ellie from the post office made scrummy jelly cakes and lamingtons (a request from Jamie) and there was a quiet little surprise when Margaret turned up with a plate of delicious Italian-style confections. My Uncle Ron paid for some wine so we could raise our glasses in an extra toast.

Suddenly it was all happening. Tiz bore the teasing about being my bridesmaid and having to wear apricot taffeta and matching shoes very well. As if! It was unusual to see her wearing a skirt rather than shorts or jeans, never mind all those dreadful trappings. She made an incredible wedding cake instead.

We woke early to a clear, fresh morning. Fifteen minutes later we couldn't see across the tidal reach for the fog. By eleven, the gods stepped in, smiled some more and borrowed a day from spring, and all was well again. The tidal reach sparkled in the afternoon sunlight. The only things missing were the dolphins and some overseas family members – and my other son, Mark. It's strange that after all these years of separation, I longed to have my English family here to witness a day I didn't think would ever happen. But I felt them in my heart and that was enough.

We stood in the cosy corner of the sitting room and exchanged our vows. The room hummed with love and joy. Cole Porter's song 'In the Still of the Night', sung by Kevin Kline and Ashley Judd, caused a few tears to be shed, but they were good tears. Again, speeches were from the heart and very revealing. Alex's perception showed clearly in his. I had told Annette that I wasn't making a speech as I had written everything I wanted to say in the books Stephen has published for me. So she read the last chapter of *Down by the River*, reminding me and others of how good life is here. Stephen doesn't often speak in public, certainly not about our personal life, but he was eloquent and gracious in all he said, especially in the tributes he paid to his previous marriages, showing his generosity of spirit.

It was a powerfully charged moment when we were presented by the celebrant as Mr and Mrs Matthews. I qualified this, though. I will always write as Brenda Eldridge, the name my parents gave me. But I am proud to be Stephen's wife. The fun and games in changing my name formally were still to come in the weeks ahead!

Of our fifty-something guests, half were family members. What a gathering. Everyone there had supported us so wonderfully through those dark days; it was particularly special that they were sharing in our celebrations. And as I always do at any celebration, in my heart, I raise my glass to toast absent friends and loved ones.

I was deeply touched by Julie, Chris's wife, who, as she left, quietly said, 'Welcome to the family.' We had a moment of kinship, the shared experience of being embraced formally into another family.

My mother had asked if we could record the wedding but this turned out to be impractical. So I sat down and wrote a sort of script and then recorded it all for her, including the vows and the speeches. Modern technology is truly amazing.

The following weekend we took all of Stephen's family to Kangaroo Island. It was years since I had been there and my eyes were opened wide yet again to the extraordinary place Australia is. I suppose seeing it through the English visitors' eyes was part of that. Even so, I have never seen mini-emus before or an enormous white turkey cock. (I like to think the turkey moved from its position in the middle of the road, otherwise no one else would have seen it either.)

A couple of weeks later we were in the post office and Ellie asked us if we had had a honeymoon. We told her about the Kangaroo Island trip but I added that I didn't think having seven other people, including three children between the ages of four and seven, with us was much of a honeymoon.

But the reality is, all our days are filled with so much laughter and contentment, and the shadow of cancer gives the brightness extra value.

Before Karyn and Joby returned to England, the subject had been raised whether we would be going to England for her wedding. Suddenly I was in chaos. Having so recently experienced the longing for my own family to witness my marriage vows, I was instantly torn in several directions.

I may have lived most of my life in Australia but part of me is forever English. I have worked out over the years since my last visit in 1996 that the England I miss is no longer there. It is my childhood I miss and the accompanying sense of security and belonging I knew. I hadn't felt these things since my dad died when I was in my early thirties. I have them again now with Stephen.

Yes, I would love to have time to sit and chat with my family, to have one last hug from my mother in a lifetime where there have been far too few 'mummy hugs'. But how to say goodbye? I have a life here. This is my home. I want to be here. The brutal fact is, if I don't go back, I don't have to say goodbye. Yes, I will miss out on the hugs, but the pain of that isn't as much as the pain of saying goodbye, knowing I will not see any of them again. As it is, I have had sixteen years to get used to the idea. If I went back to England, I would not want to leave the place again, not just my family.

Stephen has his own reasons for not wanting to go back to England. But I know he too is being torn by choices. Someone long ago taught me the expression, 'There's no such thing as a free lunch.' How true that is. For the time being at least, the decision is made that we will not go, but I have learned that nothing is ever simple and no doubt more soul-searching will happen. Like all decisions, it isn't just the final choice that is important, but also that the reasons for making it are the right ones.

Some time later, we put Tiz on The Overland on the first leg of her journey back to England and the life that was waiting for her there. There were many changes while she was in Australia. She too changed, and we had no doubt about her ability to make hard decisions and be true to herself.

For us, we now had the opportunity to re-establish our quiet life down here by the tidal reach.

Rituals

When I lived alone in the tree house for years before I met Stephen, I was also working full-time. I suppose, like many people, it wasn't till I retired that I realised how tired I used to get. I loved living among the trees in the foothills with a river running along at the bottom of the garden, but I also loved to be by and in the sea, which was about thirty minutes' drive away.

I say with a mixture of pride and embarrassment that I was forty-seven before I managed to find the courage to take my feet off the ocean floor and float. I knew the theory but had never been able to put it into practice. The time came when I decided to have a flexi-day off work and I was going to go to the beach alone and it was going to be kill or cure. A strange choice of words perhaps. Luckily for me, the ocean presented ideal conditions and it was a lovely warm day. I carefully waded out and – it happened. I floated! Oh, such bliss.

I loved that, when my ears were below the surface, I could hear my heart beating. It was, and still is, a remarkable way of being inside my body. Looking up at a moon shining in a clear blue sky while floating like this is always a wonderful feeling. Best of all was the sensation of being separate from the rest of the world.

From then on, at least once a week, no matter what the season, I drove down to the beach to play in the water. I taught myself to swim enough to be able to enjoy the water more than just floating on top. I especially love to be underwater; I just can't seem to get the breathing thing right to stay under for very long but that doesn't really matter. Someone suggested I learn how to use a snorkel but I haven't been able to get my head around the idea yet. It has something to do with the importance, to me, of being untroubled by anything. The whole point of being in the water is just being there and letting the motion, of whatever the prevailing tide, impact on my emotions.

It was years and years ago playing in rolling waves in the middle of winter that I first came eye to eye with a dolphin. What an extraordinary moment. The connection between us was unbelievable. The dolphin seemed to be smiling and yet full of compassion and encouragement for this woman who was barely holding on to her sanity a lot of the time.

My bravery is only shallow, though. I won't go out of my depth. I have to make a determined effort not to think about what might be walking on the floor of the ocean. I was bitten by a small crab once and didn't like it much and really didn't want it to happen again. Neither did I want to step on a ray. I had come close to doing that once and… It doesn't do to think too much about a lot of the stuff that gets dumped into the sea all over the world, otherwise I would never go in at all.

On reflection I can see that I stay in the water floating, paddling or swimming until I find myself laughing out loud like a child. As long as I can do that, I know deep down, where it really matters, I am all right.

Naturally when I had holidays I could go down to the beach more often. I would pack a picnic lunch, a book to read, a book to write in and off I would go for the day. I also loved to put my bicycle, Beatrice, in the boot of the car and take her down to the beach. I cycled many miles over the years, along the coast from Outer Harbour to Glenelg.

I promised myself that one day when I didn't have to go to work five days a week, I would start, if not every day, certainly as many days as possible, by riding my bike beside the sea and walking on the beach and going for a swim, if I wanted.

So here I am living in Port Adelaide and I'm retired – not from life, just from the Public Service. Three times a week after breakfast I go out on my bike. Note I don't say on Beatrice. We have a walled garden and the car lives in a locked carport, as did Beatrice. One morning, I went out to get her to go for a spin and she wasn't there! We worked out eventually that someone had jumped our high brush fence and then thrown Beatrice back over. She had gone forever. I had her for almost twenty years and felt really bereft that she was gone, probably so someone could sell her for a few dollars for who knows what kind of fix.

Such is my love of cycling and the solitude and freedom it gifts me, I went out and bought another bike, obviously called B2, but it isn't the same. Having said that, I still enjoy exploring the whole peninsula to Outer Harbour. I like going along roads I haven't been before. I carry a small shoulder bag and I'm always equipped with mobile phone, camera, a notebook and pen. Oh, and a few gold coins in case I decide to stop for a coffee somewhere.

There are many places round by the docks where the old railway lines that serviced the port when it really was a vibrant and active place have been left exposed. One morning when I was newly retired I set off for a ride and I was so busy watching a dolphin in the water I managed to get the front wheel of the bike caught in the tracks. A most inelegant fall ensued and Stephen received this plaintive call, 'I've fallen off.' He came and found me and bundled the bike and me into the car and took us home. My hero!

Regardless of the hazards of sand getting into the brake or gear mechanisms of B2, I always include in my excursions a walk or sometimes even a ride along the actual beach. I am not as brave or stupid as I used to be and now I don't go for a swim when it's cold but I often paddle my feet and end up getting soaked up to my bottom, and many are the times I have cycled home cold and wet. Stephen has stopped looking perplexed when I come in like this, just says something like, 'Been paddling?' and has been known to frown a little at the sandy footprints I leave on the mat.

Part of the wonder of going onto the beach is the walk across the dunes. It is only a short distance, but I find it's like stepping into a different world. So much wildlife clinging to and under bushes. There are signs up warning about snakes and I have seen a black one slithering across the path. Another time I saw a stumpy lizard and his mate. I have watched for ages a sparrow hawk hunting for breakfast and once a pair of them engaged in an amazing courtship flight.

For years I have heard a bird calling but not been able to see who was making such an interesting sound. It was like honey dripping. I was so pleased earlier this year to see a lovely bird sitting high on a dead twig making the call. It was almost as if he was waiting for me to take his picture. I have searched the bird books, but I am still not sure what he is, possibly one of the honeyeater family. I asked my bird-enthusiast brother, Geoff, which was a bit unrealistic as he has lived in England all his life. I had to laugh at his response explaining he would need a lot more information and a better photo and ending with a humorous reminder that guide books may be quite helpful but birds can't read and the bird might have just been visiting!

Recently I had ridden a long way and decided to stop for a coffee at the kiosk at the end of Largs jetty. I rang Stephen and invited him to join me. It was so lovely sitting together in the sun. At last, after long, long years, a little fantasy came true. Sharing this simple thing with the one I will share the rest of my life with. I wasn't stealing anything from anyone, I had the right to sit in the sun and relish living so close to the constantly changing ocean. I love that it isn't the same two days running. I love watching storm clouds and sudden squalls coming in, the sunlight reflecting silvery off aqua waves with dainty, white, lacy edges, big rollers with delicate spindrift flying high, filled with scraps of rainbows, the bright gleam of sunlight on wet sand…

Anyway on this particular morning after we had our coffee, Stephen set off back home in the car and I started to follow on the bike. Only I became distracted. There is a shop in Semaphore that sells Indian-style clothes and a wide range of other third-world items. I usually pass that way long before the shop opens, but after lazing with Stephen over coffee, the shop was open, so I thought I would pop in and see if the new stock had arrived for the coming summer. And there were wonderful things for sale. I sheepishly phoned Stephen to ask him to bring my purse over.

Stephen is so patient and seems to understand perfectly why I call this an evil shop. Our friends Peter and Joan have a second-hand bookshop which is also evil – especially the locked cabinet that has wonderful and unusual books in. I only mean evil in a light-hearted way because they relieve me of my money. I am so fortunate that these days I can spend my money on unconventional clothes and books to delight my soul. There were all those years when, for countless practical reasons, like having to feed and clothe children, it wasn't possible. As I often say to parents of young children, 'There is life after children.'

The reason I take the camera is because the world is full of amazing things. Flowers, trees, boats, birds, unusual footprints in the sand, fantastic skies and even street art. I take pictures of things that catch my attention and often write a poem to go with them and these go up on my blog (http://brendaeldridge.wordpress.com) or in my pictorial journal. I mean what is a girl supposed to do with the vision of cactus flowers leaning over an old garden fence that look like perfectly boiled eggs just waiting for a bread soldier? Or baby seagulls perched on a timber post near the bridge? And how often do you see a seal just floating in the sea waving at passers-by? Well, I accept it probably wasn't waving as such, it certainly wasn't drowning, but it looked like it was waving one flipper. Logic tells me it had something to do with balancing itself as it soaked up the sun.

The notebook and pen? Well, I am a writer after all and any writer can tell you these items are vital wherever we go. There are always notes to be jotted down for a story or poem. We daren't trust to memory because part of getting older is the holes that appear in our brains, and lovely images and ideas have a nasty tendency to fall into the holes and are never seen again. Most frustrating.

Hang on a minute! What was that back there? Brenda has a blog! Brenda who has long been called a techno-wus. Does that come with any kind of explanation? Well, we were at a poetry reading at Hahndorf with several of Stephen's writers and over coffee with Ann and Joan the topic of a blog came up. It was Ann who made it seem so achievable. So we came home and Stephen helped set it up. It didn't take long till I was well and truly hooked. Poems no longer disappeared into a folder; I put them up for other people to read. I dared myself to put up some of the paintings I had done over the years, and wrote poems to go with them. More succumbing to technology with the gift of a digital camera and suddenly it all came together.

But it didn't end there. Stephen really surprised me when he said we could reproduce some of the journal in a book. Yes, with handwritten poetry, not typed, to go with the pictures. I had the most amazing time learning how to scan from the journal and create a book. As I wrote on the blurb, I will never be Edith Holden with her *Country Diary of an Edwardian Lady*, but this was as close as I could get. *Best Heard and Seen* was yet another dream come true.

Since we seem to be in confessions-of-a-techno-wus mode, I suppose I should admit to also being on Facebook for a while. It seemed the only way I could keep in touch with a couple of brothers and childhood friend in England. They, unlike my brother Steve, aren't into writing lovely letters, or even emails. But I hated Facebook. I felt I was being drawn into this enormous electronic spider's web. Several people put up what to me were offensive and distressing images, so I decided to cancel the whole thing. Then something lovely turned up from someone else. So I disconnected from the ones I couldn't cope with and it lived for another day. But not for long. In the end, I became so tangled up with worrying about who or what I was going to see via 'friends' of 'friends' that I decided to stop doing Facebook altogether. It is a strange relief really not to feel compelled to check to see what's on there. I shall take great pleasure in finding a pen and notepaper and writing letters to my brothers explaining that it just isn't for me. Will I get replies? Probably not.

There is one last little story that goes with all the technology stuff. Once I had the blog going, Stephen re-named me Bnerda. Another one of his clever plays on words. One morning I decided to watch the dolphins from the rocky edge of the tidal reach. I put my foot onto a rock which wobbled alarmingly, lost my balance and tumbled down towards the water. It was painful and scary, as I thought I would end up in the water. I stopped just in time. I gingerly tested the bits that hurt and knew a fleeting moment of panic as I couldn't be seen from the path and no one knew I was down there, not even Stephen. Fortunately, apart from some grazes, bruises and a bump on the head, I was fine. Of course Stephen rose to the challenge and I became Bnerda the rock wobbly.

Where was I? Oh yes, my real-life cycling and being in the real world not an electronic one.

Again it's one of the little luxuries in my life to come home from a bike ride and a play in the sea and be able to step into a hot shower. When the waves have been particularly turbulent and churning up the sand, my thighs sting and itch when I get under the hot water. Or is it that my legs are cold and this is the blood getting a move on as it warms up? I don't know. As long as I don't scratch the itches, they fade quickly, but that can be quite difficult.

And then life moves on and I know Stephen is waiting for me to come downstairs. The mail must be collected from the post office and every day there are grocery items to be purchased. None of the shopping once a week that I used to do when I lived alone.

The walk also entails checking out the people in the neighbourhood. Have we seen the elderly lady walking her dogs? If not, when was the last time we saw her and is she all right? Is George the Great Dane lounging on his trampoline?

The post office has a new system and we less often get the coloured cards that tell us we have packages to be collected inside. They have larger mail boxes set aside for parcels and they leave a numbered key in our box so we can collect the packages ourselves and post the key back in a slot. It is very efficient but it means we don't get to see the girls in the post office the way we used to. We miss the opportunity to have a chat about what is going on in our lives, their lives. Efficiency is quickly demolishing the sense of country or village life that we had so enjoyed and kept us going so well.

We seem to have become people that other folk notice in our daily walks to the post office and shops. While we are watching, we are being watched. It has been commented upon that we always walk holding hands. Well, why on earth wouldn't we? One lady even calls us lovebirds. How sweet is that?

Stephen wants us to cross the road to the shopping centre at the corner of the street. It is a busy intersection most of the time and he knows I am thinking, 'Why don't we walk fifty paces along the path and go over the pedestrian crossing?' But no, he would rather suddenly announce, 'Come on, scuttle,' and I find myself scuttling to get across safely. Oh, but he does make me laugh.

Not only is he patient with my early-morning water activities, he doesn't seem to mind at all when I kick up crunchy autumn leaves on the way home from the shops. We both enjoy pausing to watch the dolphins when they are about. One day we watched a baby dolphin. It was so close to us and of course neither of us had a camera. But that didn't matter at all, we were just enchanted to witness this small creature cruising along with a protective adult, presumably mum, escorting it. We haven't seen it for ages and there was a piece in the local paper that suggested it wasn't well and hadn't been sighted by the official watchers for a while either and they doubted it had survived. Harsh reality again.

People are not the only visitors

All the while we have had visitors and marvellous events, nature has been steadily going on about her business, totally ignoring us. And what a comfort that has been.

Neither Stephen or I have considered ourselves bird-lovers, but we have become aware over the time living here that the number of different types of birds that visit our garden and the tidal reach is quite astounding. When we actually wrote them down, we had over thirty on our list.

Just for fun, I have been keeping a sort of logbook that has become out of date and I'll amend it when I'm feeling lazy and just want to sit in a quiet corner and handwrite the entries. The handwriting part is essential. It's one thing to sit here and tippy-tap quickly. At least my fingers can keep up with my mind for most of the time. But writing letters, for instance, needs to be done with a proper pen, unusual writing paper and time to go slowly. When I write to someone, I am imagining us having a cup of tea and perhaps scones with jam and cream. A ceremony that you must slow down for. Emails and text messages may be convenient but they are all too rushed for my liking.

Our garden appears to be a refuge for the birds that are challenged in some way. Oh, we have the usual squad of sparrows, and Dopey Dora (or her successor) is just one of a dozen doves that make short work of the birdseed Stephen puts out each day in the hope it will attract parrots. After three and a half years, to our utter delight, last week, three times in two days we had red-rumped parrots drinking from the bird bath that stands in the garden on the river side. They didn't stay long, just long enough for Stephen to take a photograph so we could identify them. It seems patience is rewarded quite unexpectedly.

Scruffy was part of our household for nearly a year. He was a Murray magpie and when he first turned up he had something wrong with his feet and a feather that was growing crooked in his wing. All his feathers looked disordered, hence the name. He became quite tame as we fed him breadcrumbs. The growths on his feet eventually healed themselves. It gave us so much pleasure to watch his routine of bathing and preening and then falling asleep perched up on the fence. As soon as we sat under the veranda to have breakfast or morning coffee, he would fly in and try to sit on the table.

Tiz did not share our delight in Scruffy and in all honesty I can understand why. When she first arrived to stay with us, she liked to sit in the sun on the riverside in the afternoons. Scruffy fell in love. He kept trying to get her attention, and if she had the computer on the little table he kept hovering around her till she came inside. I must confess, when Scruffy did it to me, I found it really disconcerting.

Over the winter, Scruffy disappeared for a week or more at a time. At first we thought something had happened to him, but he kept turning up. We were sure he missed Tiz because in the afternoons he strutted backwards and forwards in front of the windows till one of us fed him. He took the bread from our fingers without hesitation now. I was certain he would come indoors if we let him. Sometimes he would come to the railing at lunchtime while Stephen fed the gulls, but he didn't stay long. He seemed to have tamed his wayward feathers and looked quite sleek, except for the one crooked feather in his wing. He lost the original one but the new one grew back at the same funny angle. But although there were several other Murray magpies in the neighbourhood, some that would even pick up bread from the garden, he didn't seem to be part of the flock or to have a partner. Two regular Murray magpies were named Tidy and Suave because they really were smarter than Scruffy.

The post office, of all places, had fluffy toy birds for sale a while ago. One of them was supposed to be a magpie and if you pressed its tummy, sure enough, it sang a rather sweet little melody. We couldn't resist. We bought one for Tiz because it looked more like Scruffy than a magpie. I noticed when she was packing her things to go home that her Scruffy kept getting pushed to the side. As it turned out, there were a lot of things she really wanted to keep but wouldn't all fit so I said to just put it all in a pile and I would parcel it up and send to her. No surprise that I slipped Scruffy into the parcel. I think by the time it got to her in the middle of an English winter, she would have been glad of the reminder of the hours she spent in the sun in our garden.

Stephen has very strict procedures for feeding the gulls at lunchtime. As we have the routine of morning coffee and breakfast under the veranda when the weather is warm, so we have lunch on the balcony overlooking the water.

Stephen began throwing odd bits of bread, like the crusts of his sandwich, to the gulls. He was very impressed by their flying skills. If they sat on the grass verge in front of the house, they got nothing. He was only interested in the flyers. It's almost always windy up on the balcony and the gulls adjust brilliantly. They seem to love flying when it's gusty and we think it must be more difficult for them.

Sometimes we get those who perch on the railing and squawk. That's no good. If they don't at least fly up in an attempt to get the scraps, they are ignored and verbally abused. What! Not Stephen, surely. Well, not abused so much as insulted really. Having said that, I have known Stephen put a line of crumbs along the railing just to see how daring they will be – or how hungry.

I remember writing a poem comparing Stephen's interest in people who want to fly with the gulls flying and swooping for lunch. He has very little time for people who are 'gonna' do something but never actually do it, but seems to have almost endless patience for those who are trying to achieve a goal.

Duncan was a favourite gull for months. Duncan had lost one foot and didn't seem to manage being part of the flock, but he and Stephen had a rapport. Duncan came by again and again for pieces of bread. We used to keep count till it was about twenty in one lunchtime but he seemed to become less hungry. Why did we call him Duncan? Well, it started when Stephen noticed that after a few pieces of bread he would go down to the water in the tidal reach for a drink to wash them down. Not quite the same as dunking a biscuit in a cup of tea or coffee, but it probably had the same result for him. Needless to say, more often than not he was called Dunk for short.

Two other gulls attracted Stephen's particular attention. A one-legged gull and another with a distressingly damaged leg. It was bent at an odd angle and as he flew he often shook it as if trying to straighten it.

I wonder if birds talk to each other in some way. Earlier in the spring we had a family of magpies – mum, dad and a baby – that came at lunchtime. That in itself wasn't unusual, I suppose, but there came a time when there was only one and he seemed injured or ill. It was strange to see him trying to leap up for the bread like the gulls. Then he too disappeared and I suspect survival of the fittest had occurred.

We are now so dedicated to our bird friends that we even buy special bread for them. No, I don't mean they get the multi-seeded, high-fibre stuff but we do write specifically 'birdie bread' on the shopping list and they seem content with cheap white sliced.

Tiz wasn't the only visitor who was reluctant to sit on the balcony for lunch. People are put off, it seems, not just by flapping wings and the shadows the gulls cast, but also the droppings. Perhaps, as in some cultures it is a sign of appreciation to burp after a meal, the gulls believe leaving a message on someone's lap or lunch is the right thing to do. Hmm.

I think I get the best of things, though. When we have finished lunch and the table and chairs have been put away, the sparrows come in and pick up crumbs off the balcony. It's a bit like the swallows that sit on the railing in the mornings as if to have a quiet chat before we all get on with the business of the day. Even more reasons to count my blessings as I sit in my studio.

We still get the horrible crested pigeons in the garden bullying the other birds off the birdseed stand. But we no longer just clap our hands and shoo them away. Oh no! We have become, oh dear, I can't call it scientific exactly. We have called in the artillery. Stephen bought a water pistol. We had no idea there were so many to choose from. We ended up with one with a pump action. That worked all right till Jay, Ella's younger brother, had a try and bent something. Stephen upgraded to a much larger model that Jay was forbidden to touch. Oh, the look of longing on his face. But he is a good-natured child and gave in graciously to miserable, spoilsport grown-ups.

That water pistol didn't last any time at all and for no reason we can fathom it decided not to work. That was it: no more swishy pump action water pistols for us. Back to Kmart for the third attempt and a good old-fashioned trigger model. The pigeons still sit on the garage roof and hoot. They still try sneaking down the garage roof and flit over to the birdseed stand, but they can't help themselves, it seems, and as soon as they perch on the stand they start hooting – and of course Stephen goes out there with the new water pistol and shoots and off they go with a clatter of wings. Oh, my goodness! This is so funny. I'm certain the people who think they know Stephen well have no idea what he gets up to in the privacy of his own garden. He has been known to squirt the thing in my direction ever so casually as if it were an accident. I don't think so! I didn't raise four little boys without learning a few things. Oh, but I love this in Stephen. A staggering mind, sharp intellect, a man of great compassion and understanding, a lover of beautiful music and life in all its glory, still capable of enjoying playing with a water pistol like any nine-year-old boy.

Some months ago, we spotted a lone black swan across by the mudflats. I rather hoped he was on the look out for somewhere new for his family but he didn't stay long and doesn't appear to have come back at all. Then, the other morning I was out on the balcony watching the world wake up. The sun still hadn't risen above the hills and the sky was that beautiful pearly grey with just a hint of blue. I was stunned to see six black swans flying overhead. Their necks were stretched out long and straight and their wings had a strong, steady beat. I almost ran inside to get the camera – oh, what a picture that would be – but I knew I didn't want to miss any of this fabulous vision, so I can only hope I will remember the magic of what I saw.

Coming to the rescue

It isn't only damaged birds that find a resting place with us. We both love to walk around the garden section in Bunnings and, before it closed, our local Mitre 10. Not for us the expensive and fancy. No, we head for the rescue tables. There, for a couple of dollars, we can buy the sad-looking plants that have been left languishing.

Beside the vegetable patch and the bird bath is a small area affectionately known as the nursery. Our rescue plants stay there in their pots for a few days to see if they will recover with a bit of tender, loving care. Then we have to decide where to put them in the garden. Not always an easy decision when we are often guessing what we have bought and how tall it may grow...just small details like that.

When we first moved in, the garden was sort of all right. The standard pink roses have given us so much pleasure, especially during the dark days of the radiotherapy. They certainly lifted our spirits every time we entered the garden. My beloved round herb table in the corner seems to be perfectly at home and, because it's quite shady, the herbs do very well. I always liked the idea of growing herbs and then using them for cooking. Well, Stephen does the real cooking in our house, but I love it when he asks for herbs to go into a meal. The table is surrounded by sword ferns that bring the sense of jungle to the garden.

But we are who we are and soon the walled garden lawn area was changed. We now have a wonderful barked area where the native violets run riot and the mauve convolvulus vies for space with a ground-cover grevillea. The lavender sports flowers like purple bees beside the birdseed stand and the bushy grevillea attracts the honeyeaters. The blackbirds have taken the hint too. We often hear them singing but the plants have grown so thick that apparently it is too much bother to scuffle the bark aside in search of insects beneath. Clean, tidy paths are all very well but...

We have been given an interesting assortment of plants by friends to celebrate birthdays, book launches and our marriage. Because we do only rent we have been unsure what to do with these gifts. Large flower pots have become the answer. When the day comes and we have to move, at least we will be able to take these treasures with us. We give a big sigh of relief every year when we learn that our lease has been renewed for another year and we can put aside for a while any thoughts of having to move.

The river-side garden was a dreary place with just an indifferent lawn and a few bushes down one side. I had put some potted plants by the pillars of the balcony above, but I knew Stephen wasn't keen on them. So we decided to take things into our own hands.

Most of the lawn is now taken over by a barked garden and this has given us so much pleasure. Not just choosing the plants, but for the birds that come in now. We found a ground-cover rosemary. It has been covered in flowers for months and often during the winter while we had our breakfast indoors we watched tiny green finches feasting on the nectar. They were called Rosemary regardless of how many there were or whether they were male or female. Sometimes they go to the ground-cover grevillea with its pretty pink flowers. When we see them on that plant, they're called Greville, naturally.

Our other prize is the lotus. From a tiny sprig it has spread and spread and has masses of orange and red blooms. The honeyeaters love the flowers. I notice some tendrils have escaped under the fence and are starting to go towards the nature strip outside the garden. I watch the council guys with their weed killer sprays looking carefully at them, obviously wondering whether should they spray or not. They haven't.

The other testimony to life clinging to life is a tiny bush. I don't know what it is, but when we planted it, it was about three inches tall and even then had a couple of bright pink flowers like little tubes. The honeyeaters liked these too. But what has amazed us is the way this tiny plant has grown. It is still only small in the scheme of things, but has lots of bird-attracting flowers.

We have placed a red-glazed bird bath in the barked garden and of course Scruffy, the honeyeaters, the willy-wagtails and the sparrows have had a lovely time in it. I've noticed, while they don't mind making the water dirty with their droppings, they don't like it if I don't put fresh water in every couple of days. I'm sure there is a lesson in there for someone, but how do you toilet train birds?

Another little dream come true is the wheelbarrow on the barked garden. We searched for an old one but all we could find were big ones, the kind you find on building sites – well, you did in the old days. Then one day we spotted a child's wheelbarrow. It is red plastic but even after a few months has faded. But the plants seem to like growing in it.

For a little splash of colour along the border, we have grown petunias and pansies. I am amazed that such delicate plants can survive the harsh winds that come across the tidal reach, no doubt filled with salt from the nearby ocean. I firmly believe that plants choose where they want to grow, it has nothing to do with us. To prove my theory, we have a clump of violets growing that appeared from nowhere. Well, they were probably seeded by the ones growing next door. Just a couple of leaves at first, but now they too are spreading along the edge of the pavers.

On the other side of the garden path we had more examples of the tenacity of plants. Someone had made the strange choice of planting a date palm and this other thing that had horrible spikes on its leaves, a bit like a yukka. Tucked amongst them was a standard rose. I dug up the rose and put it in the bark garden but even with a stake it was tossed about by the wind and looked quite unhappy. I eventually and reluctantly dug it up and sent it to rose heaven. To my amazement, it sent out two new shoots among the lotus flowers. But the story doesn't end there. I notice that where it was originally, two new shoots have come up through the sword ferns.

We couldn't dig up the palm or the prickly plant and had to cut them close to the ground and put weed killer down. Even then they kept sending up new leaves for months. I am going to say we have won that battle but not with any certainty.

However, having established we can grow pretty much anything in the garden, I am a complete dunderhead when it comes to indoor plants. I love to have them. Stephen chooses some really unusual ones. Then it's a fight for survival for them as I either forget to water them for weeks or, when I remember, proceed to over-water them. Poor things. I would hate to be a pot plant living here.

I have had two victories, or should that be the plants' victories?

The African violet in the guest bedroom does seem to have thrived on neglect and currently has beautiful purple flowers on it. The other is the maidenhair fern in my studio. I almost killed it, so put it in the nursery. It started to revive, then I found little critters eating the new shoots as fast as they popped up, so it's back here in the studio doing very nicely thank you.

Will I ever get the watering thing right? I have no idea.

Travelling around a bit

It was Alex, in his speech at the wedding, who drew our attention to how much I have travelled since being with Stephen. As he rightly said, I have seen more of Australia in the past four years than I had in the previous thirty-odd.

We have been able to combine business with pleasure – well, it's all pleasure. I love the book launches. Perhaps because it was such an enormous thing for me when Stephen published my first book. Very much like sending, in turn, each of my sons on their first day of school. The launch was also my first experience of public speaking. Perhaps it is that I love to be with other writers, or being able to say to a prospective buyer, 'This is such a good read…'

I have been welcomed by total strangers with our only link being that we are writers and Stephen is our publisher. But in some ways the writers, even on first meeting, aren't really strangers. Not so much in the early days, but now I can be part of the progress of a new book from the time it lands as a manuscript on the red gum table in the cosy corner – otherwise known as Stephen's in tray. I have the super job of doing the initial preparation for a lot of the books Stephen has accepted. It is fascinating when months later I see a design for the cover for one of these books on his desk. So when I get to meet the author, I feel I do know them a little.

That we have travelled to five states to launch Ginninderra Press books is an added bonus. I do love to travel to a new place, for the journey as well as the arrival. Stephen took us to Brisbane, where we celebrated my sixtieth birthday on a paddle steamer on the river – oh yes, and met Bruce Dawe at the launch of his biography. At Newcastle we launched a book in an old gaol. It was really creepy to look in the cells and get a tiny glimpse of how awful it must have been.

I had been to Canberra several times before but with Stephen I have seen very different aspects. What a wonderful atmosphere there is in Civic, a sense of graciousness that I didn't get with the other formal government buildings. I love the mountains and the sense of always going round in circles. Easy for me: I don't do the driving.

At Shepparton and Bairnsdale in Victoria, I was given a treat travelling on country trains. It was like time had been wound back a hundred years sitting in the wood-panelled carriages and on plush seats. I have seen the horror of drought-gripped pastures with deep cracks instead of lush grasses. And I have seen tree stumps left in the ground, but the trunks had been carved with life-size figures. Amazing talent and patience.

The trains also gave me a sense of the vast distances between towns in rural Australia and how the towns had grown up around the railway stations. I was intrigued by the change to the style of houses as we left Melbourne and headed out into the country, but more telling for me was the sense of something akin to claustrophobia as we returned to Melbourne. It must be the country girl in me that still dislikes built-up areas and endless streets.

But I must acknowledge Tasmania is my favourite. We have been there several times and each time I have seen something or done something new. We took Tiz there and spent a week driving right around the island. We had a helicopter ride over Cradle Mountain and a light plane ride over Wineglass Bay. We experienced lovely warm weather and torrential rain in that brief holiday. We even stayed our last night in an old cottage built by convict labour in about 1835.

Lots of people over the years have said I would love Tasmania because it's so like England. Well, I do love it, but not for that reason. There is the sense of history, the wildness, the constant reminder of the raw challenge of nature. But the best thing for me? Trees. Whether filled with blossom and honey bees, or like ancient skeletons clinging to almost bare rock at the top of Mount Wellington, or moss-covered giants with fairy paths meandering between them, or mile upon mile of moving green just like an inland ocean or being able to touch a sequoia in the Hobart Botanical Gardens. Everywhere we went, there were magnificent trees. And of course they form green tunnels to drive through and perhaps that is the real reminder of England, or at least the part I come from.

Even in South Australia, Stephen has taken me to places I have either never been to or haven't been to for many years. Among the most spectacular has to be Wilpena Pound in the Flinders Ranges. We had recently published an anthology of poetry about The Cedars, the home of Hans Heysen, and it was amazing to see the gorges, mountains and gum trees that he had seen all those years ago and had reproduced with such skill. We had a ride in a small plane very early in the morning and, seen from up high, the mountains and the empty flat land reaching as far as the eye could see were pure magic. I also thought it fun that the pilot had to taxi the plane along the dirt runway to chase off the kangaroos just standing about and in his way for take-off.

Stephen's family gave us a very thoughtful gift to celebrate our marriage. A night in a log cabin in Stephen's favourite winery in the Clare Valley. It reminded us a bit of the cabin we had at Cradle Mountain. We both loved the silence away from people and cars. There is something about a leisurely meal under a giant olive tree on a warm spring day. Ah, it's Epicurus again. Good company, good food, good wine and good conversation.

But the part I love best about our travels is coming back to our home. Checking the welfare of the garden and birds. Knowing we will wake up to the tidal reach and the resumption of our quiet life here.

In or out of season

Since coming to Australia, I have always lived somewhere in the northern suburbs of Adelaide. I have been aware of sayings like 'We're the driest state in the driest country in the world' and that at some time in the past Adelaide and Aden were the two cities in the world where shipping would not take on fresh water – a disquieting thought. Certainly in my earlier days here, I remember water coming out of the tap red-brown and smelling strange. But above all else I have felt that the summers, most of the time, had a dry heat, a blessing for me in a way as I really don't like humid conditions.

So where have the tropical storms come from just lately? Is this part of that climate change stuff we keep hearing about? Not that I mind the rains they bring. I simply love rain at any time of year. The storms seem to pop in during the afternoon, evening and night. Obviously not early-morning risers. I watch from my studio window as the clouds build up over the ocean and gasp to see great jags of lightning coming down. And it seems some things don't change. I still instinctively cringe when the thunder cracks and rolls across the heavens above the house. Surely it will squash me if I don't duck down?

I remember as child being taught that sheet lightning wouldn't hurt me, but I had to be very careful of fork lightning. Sheet lightning was the kind that just seemed to bounce across the skies accompanying an electrical storm. The fork lightning was the serious kind that sent javelins of power to the earth as if splitting the skies. Bad enough in England where it could strike trees or a solitary barn. Here in Australia, it likes to spark grass fires which all too quickly turn into raging bushfires. That was one of the fears I had living in the foothills, that those magnificent trees would catch fire. At least down here by the tidal reach I don't have that concern.

One night we were woken by heavy thunder. A short time later when that had passed, the sky was still being lit up by what I know as sheet lightning. I walked softly into the guest bedroom and watched an amazing light show. The clouds seemed very smooth and they lit up with a colour like slightly pink-tinted cream. Now and then, a fork of lightning the same colour threw itself to the earth. There was one area to the south where the lightning was more blue and the clouds lit up with blue and silver light. I could see enough that these towering clouds were more like the ones I associate with storms. I freely admit to being relieved that there wasn't much thunder about; after all, that does rather spoil my storm-watching pleasures.

I eventually returned to our room but not to get into bed. My attention was caught by the sound of water gushing. I immediately thought of a broken water pipe somewhere, or a storm-water drain. Gradually it dawned on me it was the sound of the rain falling on the very still surface of the water of the tidal reach. I'm mystified why I have never noticed it before. Perhaps it has been hidden by the sound of the wind blowing. As I watched, I was reminded of being at the beach when a sudden shower starts. Those single big raindrops falling onto the smooth sea. There, the splashes look as if they are lace-edged. On the tidal reach in the dark, each drop sent small ripples to bump into the next one. The ripples were lit up by the street lights so it all became a mass of moving light circles and darkness. I glanced up and noticed the hazy moon, still large, though waning. It was a delightful sight.

Where was Stephen while all this was going on? He too had been awakened by the loud thunder but as things went quiet he went back to sleep. He is used to me getting up at odd hours in the night if sleep is elusive. I usually have a cup of tea and read a book for half an hour and go back to bed and sleep. As always, he put his arm round me when I slipped back into bed. All was safe in my world.

As storms approach us, the wind blasts across the tidal reach, re-arranges the plastic chairs on the balcony if we don't stack them together in a corner, and then howls and wails as it tries to come in through the screen doors. It is such a mournful sound. One winter we had some really strong winds during the night. They brought certain misgivings about whether the roof would stay on. Thus far, all is well.

The rain really does sound like someone throwing handfuls of gravel against the windows upstairs. Not wanting to be left out of the fun, the wind whips the water up into waves that chase themselves along. The Melbourne Cup has nothing on these white horses. The water has been high enough to come over the edge of the bank a couple of times since we have lived here, and I am always on the lookout in case this happens again. It's so exciting to watch the raw power of the tide.

Not so exciting when we came home one morning from a shopping trip to find the power had gone off. Of course, everything to do with Ginninderra Press is dependent on electricity powering the computers and printers. Stephen checked the iPad and found out we would be without power for a couple of hours. No problem there. He checked again a while later and the time had been extended. That was to form a pattern all afternoon. The really funny thing was the time they gave for the anticipated restarting of power. Nothing as ordinary as two o'clock or five o'clock. No, it was 1.54 then 4.56. Luckily, we have gas to cook with, so we had our evening meal as usual.

By eight o'clock, the sun was almost setting and we still had no power. It was a warm evening so we decided to go for a walk to the other side of the tidal reach in a pleasant circular route. As we walked past, we heard one of the workmen talking on the phone, saying something like, 'All will be sorted within the hour.' It just sounded so formal. By the time we arrived back home, the workmen were just packing up. They had at last fixed the problem and we had power again. It was a good reminder of how our lives are governed by these things. Oh, we spent the afternoon reading, such a hardship, but then that's the glory of a book, you don't need electricity to read it – at least during the day.

Quite a number of gardens around us have palm trees in them. I love to watch them blowing in the wind. They have their own special sound and bring a touch of the tropics into dry South Australia. Come to think of it, I rather liked the ones we had growing in the garden. The one that stood too close to the garden gate was left with a stump about two feet high when it was cut down. We planted some garlic grass in the stump and it's a bit like a fantasy garden with the delicate mauve flowers starting to appear.

My mother is always surprised when I tell her we have what, for us, are cold days and that I'm wearing three layers of clothing to try and keep warm. I even have to resort to wearing fingerless gloves during the winter as I use the keyboard.

We have to fight the cold winds as we go to the post office and there is one spot we can count on being the worst. As we walk beside the canal towards the tidal reach and take a sharp right-hand turn, we feel the bitter wind is almost able to lift us off our feet. As for all those layers of clothes, they might just as well not be there. And definitely not good cycling weather.

While our English visitors were with us, it started to rain one afternoon. The young grandchildren were playing under the carport when suddenly it began to hail. Poor Ella was really frightened by the dreadful noise and the fragments of ice hurtling down onto the lawn and let out a piercing scream. Our first thought was that she had been hurt by something. I think she was also frightened that she didn't know how she was going to get back to the house because of this wall of water. Looking at it from her perspective, her fears were very real. How quickly we forget. It didn't affect Joby the same way but then, living in England, he's used to rain and hail.

My favourite seasons will always be spring and autumn. By the time we get to the end of summer and winter, I'm longing for a change. I am lucky that my brother Steve sends me lovely letters describing his farming life and the seasons are very much the key to everything he does. So when he is talking of spring, I am having autumn and vice versa. It's like being able to enjoy them all twice.

As a pagan, I am completely at sea with the northern and southern hemisphere differences. Seasons in England were clearly defined and as a farmer's daughter I was perhaps even more aware of the weather and how it was affecting crops and animals. After all these years, I still have a problem with the winter and summer solstices. For other migrants, this probably shows itself in their difficulty with having Christmas in the blazing sun.

My vague understanding is that many years ago Christmas as a religious celebration was sort of attached to the existing pagan rituals that went with the winter solstice, the turning point in the dark winter when the days started getting longer and having more light. In the southern hemisphere, this is inside out and our summer solstice heralds the turning point when our days start getting shorter.

I have the same bewilderment over when crops are planted and harvested here, why lambs are born in our autumn and the very fact that I can grow vegetables in my garden all year providing I look after the soil properly.

But then I tell people who puzzle over my puzzling, I have been standing on my head for the past forty-odd years, no wonder I get confused. If I lived in England, I couldn't enjoy either breakfast, morning coffee or lunch, or all three in the garden all year round, as I do here. And when I think about it, there aren't really many days here that are very hot or very cold.

Seeing the light

There have always been a few logistical issues involved in living in a two-storey house with the western wall being almost entirely glass overlooking the tidal reach. One of the major ones is that the afternoon sun beats in. Most of the time this is glorious. The tidal reach turns into a river of moving sun sparkles. The reflected light can be almost blinding with its intensity. Each afternoon when we stop working – a laughable concept, as we both love what we do – Stephen and I gravitate to the cosy corner to read or do crossword puzzles. Much as we dislike shutting out this light, drawing the curtains becomes a necessity to keep out the worst of the heat.

As the sun lowers into the west, we can open the curtains again to witness staggeringly beautiful sunsets that turn the clouds and the water to crimson, soft rose pink, peach, apricot, molten gold and yellow. Heart-stopping stuff.

Stephen knows how much I love to see the new moon. Such a slender sickle of light. A steady reminder of constancy within the changes as the moon waxes and wanes. He knows too that I am superstitious and the new moon isn't supposed to be seen for the first time through glass. I have been known to walk with my eyes closed to go out of the door into the river-side garden and only open them when I'm outside.

None of this seems to bother him at all, and there have been times when he has noted the new moon before I have seen it and shows it to me. Such is my love of moon watching that I usually check her progress from the guest bedroom window. To witness a full moon glide up over the distant hills like a golden lantern is the stuff of fantasy. So is the moon making even more dramatic, silver-lined dark clouds against a night sky. When the dolphins have woken me during the night, not only do I try and see them, but I like to locate the moon before returning to bed.

Walking up the stairs to bed has become another of our rituals. We don't turn the light on. How can I describe being in the dark as we climb the stairs and then turning at the top onto the landing and being faced with our night view of the tidal reach?

The windows in the buildings on the far side are haphazardly lit up with a soft glow. So many dark spaces where there is no one living in the units. There are orange street lights and white security lights along the path and these are reflected in the tidal reach. If the water is still, they are mirror-imaged. When the water is choppy, they glitter and dance, silver and gold on black silk. The marina is lit up too, and these lights and the street lights on the arch of the nearby bridge all serve to turn the whole area into a magic grotto.

I love to check what stars I can see. Stephen loaded an application called Stellarium on my computer that enables me to see the night skies and it names the larger stars and planets. I am intrigued by the different planets that can be seen at different times and wonder how far they must travel around the universe between the times when I can see them. They have become like beloved family members, a constant presence, but some only visiting now and then.

The guest bedroom has large windows that face east and on hot mornings the sun pours in for a few hours, making the room quite like an oven. Facing east is also a wall of mirrors, the doors to built-in wardrobes. This reflects the light back into the room and I remember when we first moved in thinking this room was like a magic cave of light. I accept the practical reasons why we close the dark curtains in there on hot days but it does seem such a pity.

It is standing on the sandalwood chest by the windows that I like to watch the day wake up. Oh, all right, I confess: the windows are set high in the wall and I can only get the best view if I stand on something.

I am in awe of a sky of breathtaking loveliness. No two mornings are the same. Over the years I have written in my poems a lot about the dawn skies clothed in fantastic colours and with gold-edged clouds. And I love this blazing and glorious start to the day. But I also love to look over to the hills where I used to live and smile when they are hidden by low, rain-filled clouds. I am stilled by what I once heard called the fingers of God: those long shafts of hazy light that pour out from between the dark grey clouds with the forbidding hearts.

Thoughts to ponder over

Not every morning is visually spectacular, but a new day does herald opportunity. It is important for me to make time to meditate and pray for the courage to be able to take advantage of whatever opportunities arise to live life to the fullest.

I have been writing to remind myself of what is important to me. I have tried to add a humorous touch to keep it from getting all too serious. But I am not mocking. I am inclined to do that too often when I get a bout of self-doubt.

Stephen and I do have a wonderful life here down by the river. It is a world we have created for ourselves built on mutual love, respect and shared interests. It doesn't have to make sense to anyone else, it is right for us.

It has been said often, 'If you knew you only had six months to live, what would you do?' I know that I wouldn't do anything very different from what I do now.

I help fill our days and nights with love and laughter. I start and end my days looking out of our bedroom window, seeing the tidal reach and saying quietly, 'It's still out there…'

There's a Rainbow Serpent in my Garden

Opening the garden gate

I've discovered there's a Rainbow Serpent in my garden. It's a discovery that in a very dramatic way has changed me and the way I see things. Being a new discovery, it still feels rather strange and, in my usual way of writing things down to make them real, I hope to clarify some misconceptions I've had and identify some fears, and so understand them better and make some headway in overcoming them.

Turning over old ground

Gardens have always been important to me. I grew up on a farm in a small English village called Forty Green. Our garden was quite large and given over mostly to growing vegetables, with a small patch of lawn and some flower beds. I was even more fortunate that I had an extended garden – the orchards and meadows belonging to the farm, and beech woods just across the lane. It was a safe haven for any child to grow up in but particularly for this nature child who had little interest in social norms and cared far more about flowers than people.

Marriage and motherhood took me away from Forty Green. At twenty-one, I was stepping onto the soil of Australia as a very green migrant and I have lived in the Adelaide suburbs since then. I heard someone say once that Australia is just a big sandpit in the ocean and I never questioned it. I was aware that most of the population lived close to the coast and, if I considered it at all, thought that the vast interior was empty red desert.

My marriage of twenty-one years turned out to be a difficult business and I was so intent on looking after my four sons, keeping my sanity and spiritual self intact, that I had no room for thoughts about this place I called home. I had no capacity for, or interest in, reading its history or its literature and no desire to go exploring. My travelling was all on the inside, learning who I was and what I believed in.

I did have one thing I was sure of: I was meant to be here in Australia. Since seeing the Adelaide Hills when I first stepped off the plane, I felt a kinship with the 'sleeping dragon' that the hills put me in mind of. Two trips to England over the years proved that I no longer belonged there. It's strange therefore that I have never wanted to buy a house and claim ownership of a piece of land here. As circumstances would have it, my name does appear as the 'owner' of the plot of land where my son is buried, but that is his place not mine. The feeling of being meant to be here has been reinforced by the birth of two of my grandsons, who have a part-Aboriginal mother.

I only ever had one dream of my own – to be a published writer – and Stephen has made that dream come true, several times over, since he entered my life. As I have written in *Down by the River* and *It's Still Out There*, we moved into this rental house beside the tidal reach in Port Adelaide within weeks of our first date. We love the various birds that frequent both the tidal reach and our garden, where we put seed and breadcrumbs out for the likes of the sparrows, doves, seagulls, Murray magpies and blackbirds, and we grow native, flowering bushes for the honeyeaters.

I refer to the back garden as our walled garden, as it's surrounded by a high, if only brush, fence. It's small and we work in it together. We've spent a lot of pleasurable hours making it into a native garden with stepping stones running between the bushes and ground-cover plants. We sit under the veranda to have our morning coffee all year round and from spring to autumn we have our breakfast out there too. I cherish the sense of privacy and seclusion away from the rest of the world. I love to sit in the garden to write in my journal or letters to friends and family. As I have said many times, I am a compulsive writer.

I was able to retire from the public service shortly after my sixtieth birthday and since then, living with Stephen in this quiet haven, I have let go of much anger, grief and fear. We have travelled from Brisbane down the east coast and along the Great Ocean Road and to my favourite, Tasmania, either to book launches or for holidays, and I have loved every moment of it. I've discovered I love travelling and seeing new places.

I've always been an avid reader and gradually with Stephen's encouragement I started reading about Australia and its history. Xavier Herbert's *Capricornia* and *Poor Fellow My Country* were the first. And I was hooked. *Poor Fellow My Country* encapsulates brilliantly in 850,000 words the majesty and tragedy of Australia and the Aboriginal people. Yes, a big book but a big and complex subject.

With stability in my own life for the first time since I'd left Forty Green, I was beginning to develop the ability to see beyond my own troubles. Stephen found out about a tour package that would take us by air to Darwin, give us two days in Kakadu and a day exploring Darwin and then bring us back to Adelaide on the Ghan, with whistle-stops at Katherine Gorge and Alice Springs. Yes, I was ready for this. I was apprehensive about what I'd find but knew I had the courage, albeit a bit wobbly, to face this journey with an open heart and mind.

Why an open heart and mind? Because among my fears is one of Aboriginal people. My early experiences of them were at the front counter of Salisbury Department of Social Services (later Centrelink), where I quickly learned I was meeting people at their most vulnerable.

For as long as I can remember, I've used direct eye contact to make a connection with someone. In the work situation, if I made eye contact, it seemed to give most people some assurance that I wasn't only an uncaring face of the government insisting they fill out great piles of forms to receive a despised handout. But when I tried to make eye contact with Aboriginal people, I was shocked by the contempt and desperation I was faced with and I stopped trying.

I'm also superstitious and, while I knew almost nothing of Aboriginal mythology and laws, I had heard of pointing the bone and singing someone to death and I was terrified I'd do the wrong thing, even unintentionally, and that would be my fate.

Now I was going to be venturing deep into the traditional home of the Aboriginal people. Why on earth would they want to make me feel welcome?

Digging new ground

We set off late in November. The flight from Sydney to Darwin took just over four hours. The little screen on the seat in front showed our progress and our speed between seven hundred and eight hundred kilometres per hour. I was beginning to get a sense of the distance we were travelling across Australia. I kept watching out of the window. I wanted to see the red desert I'd imagined. It wasn't like that. All I saw were endless tracts of nondescript grey-coloured earth, which was probably vegetation of some kind, and a million creek beds that from a height of thirty-something thousand feet looked empty, just slightly darker in colour than the rest. I was reminded of the Ordnance Survey maps we used to study in high school in another lifetime.

The long, long, ruler-straight roads that I could see were of red earth and every now and then several would meet up. There was no obvious reason from this height but they did make interesting patterns among the swirls and twirls on the ground.

The clouds started to build up as we neared Darwin and for a few moments we had a bumpy ride. Down below, things were getting far more interesting. Not the rich verdant green I expected in the tropics but certainly green – and proper rivers. Already I could see that they really do wind across the land like snakes.

The coastline around Darwin is made up of bays and inlets, and it was impossible for me to work out where we were in relation to the city itself. What I did notice was the fan shape of orange/brown that stained the aqua water where a river flowed into the sea. I'd seen it countless times in pictures, but this was real!

Darwin airport reminded me a little of Hobart, the same country town atmosphere, I think. It was raining and warm. The air-conditioned bus took us into the city along a frangipani-lined highway. The frangipani looked beautiful and relaxed, not like the strained ones I see in Adelaide gardens, where I suspect the climate is too dry for their comfort. We checked into our hotel and, as we had been promised, we had a view to the west over Darwin Harbour.

The water was only about fifty metres away across a parkland area running the length of the Esplanade. Soft green grass, big tall trees – a couple with scarlet flowers – and bougainvillea trailing over fences. I hoped we would witness a tropical sunset later. But the idea of paradise was quickly dispelled when we learned that Cyclone Alessia was on her way. Apparently she was brewing off the west coast and heading towards Darwin, due to arrive late the next day. I was relieved knowing we were going south-east to Kakadu first thing in the morning and hopefully out of harm's way.

We went for a walk in search of somewhere to have our evening meal and it was evident that the harsh reality of life for the local Aboriginal people was the same as it is for the ones I see every day. Behind the hotel there were a few very much the worse for alcohol gathered in the walkway leading from the transit centre (really nothing more than a large bus shelter) to the main street. I was frightened as we scurried past.

There was an old man sitting on the pavement. I looked away as we passed him. I admitted this weakness to Stephen and he commented that he had looked into those eyes – and wished he hadn't.

After a delicious Thai meal, we headed back to our hotel in time to watch an enthralling sunset of great billowing grey clouds with peach and apricot edges.

A heavy clap of thunder pulled me abruptly from sleep. I lay in bed waiting and listening for the next and the room was lit up by the flash of lightning. I glanced at the clock. It was almost time to get up anyway, so I decided to look out of the window. It was still very dark and another flash of lightning made me flinch. The thunder grew louder, so I hid in the bathroom with the excuse of having a shower. Some fears are not so easy to overcome.

Shortly after six, we stood at the transit centre waiting for our coach to take us to Kakadu. We watched a couple of policemen checking out broken windows in the walkway. No leap of imagination to conclude how they had ended up that way.

It was already warm, and raining steadily but not heavily. This was the first of many times the thought crossed my mind, what is a girl from Forty Green doing here?

I wasn't the only one doing some wondering. Stephen came from the south-west of England to Australia in 1979 with his young son, who was then not quite eight. They lived for a while at Daly River, a few hundred kilometres south-west of Darwin, where Stephen was principal of the tiny school for a time. This meant he had the advantage of knowing what the climate was like.

He found Darwin itself changed almost beyond recognition. When he was here, it was still rebuilding after Cyclone Tracy blew most of it away at Christmas 1976. Although he hadn't been to Kakadu before, there were going to be many things that would remind him of his time here all those years ago.

For me, it was going to be like colouring in blank spaces. I've always sensed Stephen isn't comfortable talking about his experiences living in the far north and I hadn't been able to imagine what it was like for him. I began to see that this trip was going to bring back into focus the enormousness of his decision to come to Australia with a child and start their life here in a remote area. So often we do things when we are younger, with untried courage, following some instinct we're barely aware of. It feels right and so we keep going on. It can be very frightening when years later we look in retrospect at what we have achieved.

Ted was our driver and guide during our two-day Kakadu experience. Those two days will influence me for the rest of my life. Ted had a reverence for this land like I've never sensed in anyone before. His father was one of the Stolen Generation and ended up on Tiwi Island off the coast of Darwin, where he still lives. Ted had a wonderful, dry sense of humour and kept us entertained with anecdotes and stories. He was full of information about history, the airfields, gaols and new suburban development as we drove down the Stuart Highway, then we turned left onto the Arnhem Highway and I felt our journey really begin.

Mile after mile of trees – savanna woodland, not tall eucalyptus trees. This was no pathway through green tunnels like Tasmania. The leaves were not like the blue/grey ones we see in South Australia. Not like the English beech woods I remember and love so much with their mysterious depths and towering canopy. These trees had fresh-looking leaves with a touch of yellow in the green giving them a wonderful lightness. This savanna had a calming effect on me. I knew it was something that would heal damaged emotions.

Termite mounds I'd seen in documentaries and movies were here for real. There were great tall sentinels standing back from the roadside. There were dinky small ones with smooth rounded tops standing close to the edge of the road like naughty children waiting to dash across, and all sizes between. There were even some leaning up against trees and signposts.

It was barely out of the dry season, but there'd been enough rain to form large stretches of water as we approached the Mary River. This meant we were surrounded by birds. Side by side a brolga and a jabiru! I'd never seen either before other than in pictures. I came to love the jabiru, or black-necked stork. We saw a lot of them over the next couple of days. It's the only native stork in Australia and the sun on their necks made them gleam dark green/blue and their legs were bright pink. You could wonder why the name black-necked stork. The jabiru is also the symbol for vigilance. (Time for a confession which will come as no surprise to those who know us. When we arrived back in Darwin from Kakadu, we did what we always do and checked out book shops. I found a fascinating book called *Animal Dreaming* that tells me about the symbolic and spiritual language of Australasian animals.)

White egrets were everywhere, some small, others much larger than the ones we are used to on our tidal reach, and the ibis were slightly different from the ones we know. Ducks aplenty too – not like the ones here: these were whistling or brown ducks. But the magpie geese were definitely Ted's favourite. They were beautiful to look at and to watch in flight, but Ted loved them to eat!

We pulled in at Bark Hut for a comfort stop and a quick coffee. It's a camping area and I should think a popular place to pause before entering the Kakadu National Park. We were issued with passes to go into the park and Ted emphasised the importance of carrying them with us. Apparently the rangers do spot checks and I suppose it would be embarrassing and costly not to have one.

I felt we were being drawn into a world that inspired reverent silence. Was this being instilled by Ted or our own instincts? Perhaps both. I remember a similar feeling in Tasmania when we drove down a long, winding, narrow road between enormous trees that made me feel we were going along the veins of a living creature.

Ted drove us past the Aurora Kakadu Resort where we'd be staying that night and on to the Nourlangie art site. By now the sky had cleared and the sun was shining and it was getting hot. I began to realise the importance of having drinking water with us at all times. We clambered along a path up to a rocky outcrop with overhanging parts providing a deep shelter beneath. I didn't know what to expect and was flabbergasted, not just by the paintings themselves, but by the fact that they'd been there for thousands of years and were undamaged by the elements.

Trying to describe rock art is foolish. Oh, I could talk of what they call X-ray art. The Aboriginals were so familiar with the insides of the animals they killed to eat that they depicted vital organs inside their paintings. I could talk of the story the artwork tells and the colours and how they made the paint, but none of that means much till you come across these figures in the vast expanse of the land. There are thousands of these sites hidden within Arnhem Land.

I wondered why the paintings were there and Ted couldn't give us more than a speculative answer but, as Stephen pointed out, it could well have been a means of entertainment. When the rains come, whole areas are completely cut off for months and there must have been limits to what the people could do to while away long days. Another possibility was that they were leaving pictorial messages for other tribes passing through – barramundi and wallabies indicating a good food source available in the area.

But there's the traditional story among the Bininj/Mungguy people about the Creation Ancestors and the Mimi spirits who they believe were the first to paint on rock. The Rainbow Serpent is a powerful ancestor known to many Aboriginal groups across Australia and here in Kakadu she's said to have formed the passages through rocks and formed waterholes. She's part of the life cycle of plants and animals and the seasonal changes.

There's so little we know or will be told of the Aboriginal people and their ways and it's to break a sacred trust to intrude with our questions. We can only accept what they choose to share with us. I loved this concept of a snake making the space for waterways and in turn sustaining all life.

I felt too that Ted was sharing a precious gift as he told us about the Creation Ancestors while he escorted us through this place.

Even on that short walk through the bush, I was aware of the stillness and the silence that is no silence. The constant rustle of leaves, an occasional bird call and the chirring of cicadas that rose and fell in volume like the strains of some hidden orchestra. When anyone spoke, it was with a hushed voice as if afraid to disturb something or someone.

Before driving us away from Nourlangie, Ted took out a didgeridoo and walked the length of the bus playing it, swaying it from side to side as he went. It was almost like a cleansing ritual. Then he brought us back to the present by driving us to Gagudju Lodge, Cooinda. I'm just showing off: Gagudju is the native pronunciation of Kakadu.

Ted told us about the importance of fire. The grasses are burned by the Aboriginal people to promote new growth, which in turn brings in animals. He showed us a short movie that explained how they can do a cold burn, which only moves slowly and gives the animals time to escape without being charred.

I must be honest now and admit to being glad Stephen had bought me sensible shoes. When I confirmed our booking for the tour, I was advised to wear sensible clothing, to prevent getting sunburned, and sensible shoes. I was in trouble. I only ever wear sandals and, under protest, sneakers when riding my bicycle. I muttered and snarled as we went out in search of sensible shoes and a sun hat that I could scrunch up into my bag when not being worn. It was money well spent. I could walk safely over the jagged rocks and Stephen was more or less at ease, not forever on the alert in case I twisted an ankle or lost my footing. I have a history of slipping and falling on rocks. What does it say when I'm pleased to submit to doing the sensible thing? Not the end of the wild child, I hope!

At Cooinda we were provided with a wonderful selection of cold meats and salads for lunch, and fruit to follow. We sat out in the open courtyard with a canopy to protect us from the sun. There was something magical about sitting in the heart of the bush, drinking sparkling wine, feeling sublimely at one with the world around me and sensing it was the same for Stephen.

Ted collected us up – there were twenty-four in the group – and drove us to Yellow Water. The lagoon spread around us, a haven for birds, and when the rains came it would stretch over many square kilometres. If I'd been impressed by the bird life on our way to Kakadu, this was going to be magnified beyond measure.

The cruise boat was like a large tinnie able to carry up to thirty-six people. That might sound fine, but our guide, a softly spoken Aboriginal woman, quickly pointed out the first of many estuarine or saltwater crocodiles we were going to see. We'd been informed that because it had been raining a bit we might not see any crocodiles. I was intrigued when she told us her mother was among those who record the movement of the crocodiles, becoming quite familiar with different ones, recognising them mostly by their injuries. The aluminium boat seemed very frail to me as we floated so close to one I could have reached out and touched it – if I'd been utterly stupid. It was three or four metres long and seriously scary. The warning to keep our arms inside the boat was easy to heed.

The guide was wonderful. Like Ted, she took pride and delight in sharing her world with us and was keen we should see as much as possible, giving us the opportunity to appreciate her world. Such eyesight. Even allowing that this was her home territory, she amazed us again and again with her ability to spot birds and I felt she was introducing us to her friends or her family. It was easy for us to see jabiru, egrets, magpie geese, pigmy geese and spoonbills – after all, they were big enough to spot easily and there were so many of them. But how on earth did she spot the solitary tiny kingfisher? Not only that, she reversed the boat and, without disturbing the bird, went close enough for us to take photographs.

There was a white-bellied sea eagle perched majestically in a tree, and a few minutes later we saw two more. My *Animal Dreaming* book says they're spirit guides. I like the sound of that. But the best was the jacana, which is like a small moorhen. They have similar big feet and run about on the lily pads. They're also called Jesus birds – it must be the walking on water thing, I suppose.

I haven't described the lilies: big pink and white flowers among large green leaves in great swaths on the water and of course the large salt and pepper shaker type seed pods. Wild horses, pigs and buffalo had almost trampled these beauties out of existence but with the culling of the animals the lilies are recovering. They were so exotic and added much to the general tranquillity.

Back to the jacana. Our guide had seen him a few days previously and she said the babies were about a week old. What babies? Well, there were four of them and he had them tucked under his wings. He? Yes, he. Once the eggs have hatched, mum goes off on secret women's business and dad is left to look after the babies till they can look after themselves. As he became agitated by our presence, he began dropping the babies. They were about the size of my thumb and so agile – and sooo hard to see.

We were taken back to the landing and I think it was safe to say we were all a bit dazed by what we'd seen and felt. Not too bemused, though, to spot a tiny green finch as it hopped among the bushes beside the boardwalk.

But a different reality awaited us.

Stephen and I chose to go on a scenic flight that lasted almost an hour and we'd meet up with Ted again in the small township of Jabiru at the Gagudju Crocodile Holiday Inn. Apparently from the air the inn looks like a giant crocodile.

A brief geography lesson here. There's a gigantic sandstone escarpment that divides Kakadu and Arnhem Land. It's hundreds of kilometres in length and rises to about three hundred metres now. The escarpment has eroded a great deal since it was formed. It's a riveting sight, so deeply orange/red, rising high above the rich green of the trees below.

The pilot took six of us to a small airstrip and we were off. We soared over the wetlands of the Yellow Water and could see clearly how it would be transformed from lagoon to vast floodplain when the rains really set in. The birds and crocodiles would spread further too, so we were lucky to see them before more rain fell.

All the while we were flying, we could see three quite separate storm fronts. They were dark blue/grey and where the rain was falling they had an almost vertical edge to them, coming down to the ground. The pilot said he could just fly round or between them so there was no danger of us getting caught in a heavy squall.

Gradually we travelled back over the savanna woodland and all the while the distant looming escarpment was getting closer. We saw hidden billabongs that have water in them all of the year. We flew along the front of the escarpment, over Nourlangie, and then turned to fly a little way over Arnhem Land itself.

The change in the terrain in Arnhem Land was unbelievable. In this area at least, it's just rock, criss-crossed with very straight lines that are actually gorges. I have no idea how, but trees grow in them. From up in the air it looked very inhospitable and, to me, a bit like an old kitchen chopping board with knife marks across it. Yet there are some Aboriginal people who live there all of the time. When they're cut off by floods, foodstuffs are flown in to them. The pilot actually said 'supermarket items'. This was one of a few discordant notes I felt in our whole trip. The cynic in me asked why they would want anything flown in if they wanted to live the traditional way. But it's not for me to make a judgement. Their reality is so different to mine.

The next discord really jarred and I find it very difficult to reconcile. The pilot flew us past what he claimed is the most sacred place of all along the escarpment. (I don't know the veracity of this claim; he was not of Aboriginal descent and no one else mentioned it and I certainly wasn't going to ask.) Yet literally five miles away is the Ranger uranium mine.

This place is an obscenity. An enormous hole in the ground, great mounds of rock and earth and an artificial lake. The first mine is being re-filled and this, the second one, will also be, in time. There are plans for a third mine but that's still under negotiation as it would not be an open-cut mine like the first two.

There are very complex issues here between the traditional owners of the land, their survival in a modern world and the pressure upon them to give permission for their sacred home to be desecrated for some supposed greater need.

(The mining company have made great claims to monitor constantly for anything that could damage the environment. I was sickened when we returned home to learn that a million litres of acidic radioactive slurry had leaked from a tank. Apparently this was the latest in a number of incidents that have seriously eroded the trust of the traditional owners. Needless to say, the negotiations for the third mine have come to an abrupt halt.)

We landed at the Jabiru airfield and were driven to the town of Jabiru, built at a cost of eighty million dollars to provide all the needs of the miners. Sixty-two million dollars were provided by the mining company. With an outlay like that, I find it hard to comprehend how much profit they expected to make. The original vision for the town didn't work out as expected and now there are only about twelve hundred people living there. I was pleased that we could just get on the coach and be driven back to the Aurora Resort.

What an oasis within an oasis it turned out to be. The rain was back and it was hot outside, but our room was cool. A disconcerting notice in the bathroom told us that the frogs and geckoes that could come up through the drains only eat insects so please would we leave them alone. And another sign requested we keep the screen doors closed as there were 10,000 different kind of insects in the neighbourhood. No problem.

We walked in the pouring rain to the dining room, marvelling at the flowering trees and bushes, and thoroughly enjoyed a whisky each before tucking into locally caught barramundi followed by mango cheesecake. It really was scrumptious washed down with a bottle of lovely sparkling wine. It was slightly incongruous, though: tablecloths with Aboriginal dot painting designs, heavy cutlery and classic white crockery and yet here we were hundreds of kilometres from Darwin and so-called civilisation. When the tour brochure said we'd spend a night in the wild, I'm not quite sure what I had expected.

As we walked back to our cabin, the warm night air was filled with the sound of the cicadas. It seemed the corellas had settled for the night while we had dinner. Despite the hum of the air conditioner, it was quiet and easy to sleep.

More digging

We woke early as usual and headed back to the dining room for breakfast. It was raining, so no good looking for a brilliantly coloured sunrise.

As we were in the coach almost ready to leave, a dingo trotted across the car park. I didn't quite believe my eyes and asked Ted and, yes, he had heard it calling down by the billabong during the night. What a start to our day.

We were off to the East Alligator region. There are no alligators in Australia. The white explorer who came through here knew about alligators but not crocodiles. He mistakenly called it the East Alligator River and for some weird reason the name has remained unchanged.

There have been lots of times when I have been impatient with the Australian laid-back, laconic attitude of 'She'll be right, mate.' After only a few hours in the Northern Territory I learned that rushing about just isn't viable. I've long loved the lines from the poem 'Leisure' – 'What is this life if full of care, we have no time to stand and stare…' – and I do this a lot. What I found here was different. It must have something to do with distance and heat. You just can't muck about with either. If you injure yourself out in the bush, or get dehydrated, there's no quick fix. Knowing some bushcraft skills isn't quirky and amusing, it can mean the difference between life and death. It takes time even with planes or helicopters to come and find you and transport you to a hospital. That's if you can get a message out that you need help in the first place.

Today we were going to Ubirr art site and then on a cruise along the East Alligator river. Bemused as I was already, it's easy to understand now why this day would have such a profound effect on me.

We arrived at the gates to Ubirr only to find them still locked. Rather than just sit and wait for the ranger to come and open them, Ted drove us to nearby Cahills Crossing, the only road access across the East Alligator river, which forms the divide between Kakadu and Arnhem Land. The river was orange/brown in colour and there were tall trees on the banks on either side. We were warned not to go too close to the edge because saltwater crocodiles are known to jump to attack.

The flood marker showed the level of the water was 1.2 metres and when a four-wheel drive and an ordinary sedan pulled up it was obvious they could not cross. The river is tidal but the additional fresh water feeding into the river from recent rain meant that any tidal fall might not be enough to allow anyone to cross. The occupants of the vehicles this day were Aboriginal people going back into Arnhem Land and I wondered what would happen if they couldn't get home for months. They seemed a little perturbed but they didn't get uptight or anxious – more of a laconic shrug. (We learned later that only the day before the crossing had been easy to get over.)

We also went part of the way along the Manngarre walk. We were still going along the banks of the river but behind a wire netting fence. Our education came from the fruit bats hanging in the trees and flying about. They were so noisy and like something quite prehistoric in appearance. I'd seen some before on the Gold Coast among the trees in shopping precincts, but they were very different out here in their natural habitat.

By the time we drove back to the gates, they'd been opened.

Ubirr is a rocky outcrop with quite a steep climb to the highest point and along the way there's more rock art. We were walking along a twisting path in the warm rain that was gentle to the senses. Then around a bend and we were suddenly looking at figures on the rock face. This is where time as we measure it becomes irrelevant. Well, more than time: people too. These paintings had been put there thousands of years ago or it could have been yesterday. OK, big deal. Except nothing else shows any sign that people have been here. Everything is untouched, unscarred: no buildings, no monuments to proclaim how 'clever' we are. For once, people had really got it right in their connection with the land (except for the bloody uranium mine).

As a writer, I wondered if this was their way of saying, 'We are here.' In the northern hemisphere we read about the wandering bards of old, spreading oral history, and they were news carriers too, honoured by everyone. With the introduction of paper, this role has been handed over to poets and other writers. Perhaps the painters were trying to extend their oral history and storytelling. Or were they like shamans, having an extra gift?

I've been reading a little about Aboriginal culture and came across something that resonates with my own thoughts: that they had the ability to communicate on a different level, like telepathy, so they didn't need to have a written history. I wonder if, because this concept is so alien to white people, it has been denied credence. How can you explain the unexplainable, for such is the nature of this kind of communication? Hard enough in the same language; impossible, I should think, across a language barrier. And so it has been rubbished and ridiculed out of our ignorance and fears and our unwillingness to admit that 'natives' could know more than us.

Now I'm coming close again to my fear of making eye contact with Aboriginal people. I believe something deeper than my thoughts can be read by eye contact and perhaps my fear is of what can be seen in my eyes. Once a connection is made, I believe the link is always there and I am ever vulnerable. There's more to this that I'll come back to.

We continued our climb up the rocks. They were interesting too. It was a bit like walking up steps with every flat surface covered with indentations, some like saucers and some much larger, where the rain and wind had worn the rock away. There was captured water in all of them. The rain was still softly falling; there was a gentle breeze; the air was warm, almost tangible.

Nothing had prepared me for the view from the top. Awesome took on its true meaning. We turned 360 degrees and, as far as the eye could see, there were trees, the floodplains, the red sandstone escarpment and in the distance blue/purple mountains. I felt as if arms were holding me in an all-encompassing embrace. I accepted the gift yet even now I wonder at, but do not question, the comfort in such vastness. The absence of people and their negative vibrations had much to do with it.

I wish Ted hadn't told us that a scene in the *Crocodile Dundee* movie had been filmed here. Was that supposed to give the area street cred or something? There again, he was probably trying to appeal to a wide range of visitors or possibly introducing a touch of levity to help get us focused before the next adventure. He also showed us a plume of smoke coming from among the trees. That was our Aboriginal guide for the river cruise and his mates having a barbecue beside the landing.

As we pulled into the parking area, one of these men approached us carrying a plate loaded with his lunch. He was not pleased to see us and certainly didn't welcome the interruption. I felt a pang of angst that stayed with me for a while, even though it was a different man, Robbie, who was to be our guide.

Our cruise boat was the same large tinnie type we had on the Yellow Water. The river seemed to be running quite fast to me. No sooner had we pulled away from the landing than Robbie spotted saltwater crocodiles. The banks of the river were steep but that didn't seem to trouble them at all. It's an odd sight to see a large tail stretching almost vertically up the bank while, at the other end, a gaping mouth shows lots of teeth close to the water.

Robbie stopped the boat midstream and came up to the front where we were sitting. He had the softest voice and he looked me in the eye and began to talk about the different things they can do with pandanus, stringy bark trees, ironbark trees and the native hibiscus.

I was stunned.

We went further along the river and he stopped again to show us some grasses on the bank. Spears are made from the tall, hollow stems. Again he walked up to the front of the boat and sat in front of me and looked directly into my eyes as he spoke.

It was as if he was testing his audience in some way too, because gradually he revealed a wonderful, quiet sense of humour.

A bit further and this time when he paused and sat near us he had a piece of sandstone and a small piece of ochre. He wet the sandstone and made the ochre paint used for the rock art. He gently daubed a stripe onto the backs of our hands. I felt we had been accepted. This feeling was reinforced when he approached a rocky outcrop on the Arnhem Land side of the river.

At the beginning of the cruise, Robbie had told us that we weren't allowed on Arnhem Land without permission. Now, he said we could step onto his land for ten minutes and we could take photographs. As he steered the boat to the bank, a metre-long young crocodile slithered into the water with a splash. I didn't actually see it myself, but it caused a stir among a few of the ladies, who had been startled by its agility.

There was a billabong close to the river, and standing on the bank was simply extraordinary. It was so still and dark green, so different to the running river. It was as if the world had paused. Stephen knew a few anxious moments because I'd blithely forgotten the warnings about crocodiles and had just walked over, pushing through some bushes, to get close to the billabong.

We were shown a dent in the rock where the points of spears had been rubbed sharp. That must have taken a lot of spears over a lot of years!

We returned to the bank where the boat was moored. Robbie had placed four or five spears upright in the ground. He showed us one that had four barbs lashed to the end. This was a spear used for punishment. There's a strict and, to me, complicated set of laws about who can marry into which tribe and, if you break the law, this spear is thrust into the culprit's thigh. You cannot pull this spear back out; it has to be pulled right through. Stop and think about that a bit. The effects would be far reaching. How would you keep up when the tribe decided to move on? How could you hunt? As Robbie said, you could be seen limping and the women would know you couldn't be a good provider. Rough justice.

Robbie explained that they can't strike rocks together to make a flame. They have to rub sticks together and the flame is then transferred to the inside of the stem of the pandanus where it will smoulder for weeks. They can carry the fire wherever they go.

He also showed us a rock from which very sharp small shards could be broken off. Among other things, they're used to cut themselves for ritual scarring. He grinned at me when he said it hurt like having a tattoo done. Had he seen the tattoo of oak leaves I have on the top of my shoulder?

A woomera is made from the ironbark tree and has a barb lashed to one end. This barb is placed in the end of the spear to give it extra power. Robbie gave us a demonstration, sending his spears far across the river. He was a showman too and he paused and counted to three before he threw each spear so we could take photographs. He had such a lovely smile, which revealed a tooth missing. Somewhere, years ago, I'd been told this is part of initiation.

Robbie took us further along the river between the towering sandstone cliffs. He stopped talking. In the silence I wept a few silent tears but I'm not sure if there was a specific reason. This was truly a magical place and I felt a deep stillness settle within.

On the way back, Robbie collected the spears that were still floating on the surface. As we slowly approached the landing, he thanked us for being on the cruise but, more importantly, he thanked the spirits of the place for allowing us to be there. It was a deeply moving moment. There was one more brief eye contact. His were full of compassion and something akin to approval.

He told us the word for goodbye in his language but I didn't feel right using it. I noticed Stephen didn't either. Robbie shook us all by the hand as we left and accepted Stephen's and my English thanks.

I asked Ted about punishment for the girls who had gone along with the breaking of tribal law. He wasn't comfortable answering. The older women were the ones who administered this punishment and they would probably have beaten her with a stick on her collarbone. Men aren't permitted to see women's blood. When I thought about that a bit, how hard would it be to gather food, cook, tend the needs of babies if your collarbone or arm was broken or damaged? I noticed too, that Aboriginal men don't like to talk about anything to do with women's business.

We were driven back to Jabiru and the Crocodile Inn for lunch. I think we were all suffering from information overload to our senses. I know I certainly was.

Afterwards, on the three-hour drive back to Darwin, it was good to just sit quietly and contemplate my new awareness of the importance and significance of water. If we had been one day later, we would not have left Darwin because tours were cancelled due to the threat of the cyclone. If we had been one day later, the Yellow Water wetlands would have been much more widespread because of rain and we would not have had the concentration of birds and crocodiles to see. One day later and the East Alligator river cruise might have been cancelled because of the stronger current and higher water levels. The gods or the spirits of this land were watching over us.

Seeing the Aboriginal people in their own environment, witnessing their quiet dignity, their soft voices and gentle humour, making eye contact with me, all of these things helped me understand better the appalling plight of the ones I had previously encountered. When they or their ancestors were driven from their land, they lost more than their homes, they lost their whole social structure and their sense of themselves.

Having glimpsed the world that was once theirs, I know why it's right for me not to look into their eyes. How dare I be so rude.

There have been things in my life that my mind just cannot get to the edges of. The horror that the Aboriginal people have experienced since outsiders came to this land is one of those things. I will not presume to know how they feel. I can only draw on my own feelings of displacement and dislocation coming to this country as a migrant; my own fight for survival as an individual determined to be true to myself.

As we left Kakadu behind us, I thought at first that I was going to be released from the wonderful soothing embrace of the wilderness. I was wrong. My heart knows something not known before. The words in Desiderata – '…you are a child of the universe, just like the trees and the stars you have a right to be here…' – are no longer something to cling to in the hope they're right. I have been truly accepted here by the spirits of this land.

We were the last people to get off the coach and when we said goodbye to Ted, I believe he knew something very special had occurred. There was something in his handshake with Stephen, the hug I received, that went far beyond being just the end of another tour.

Community gardening

Stephen had mentioned before that when he lived at Daly River, there were times when only a cold beer would touch his thirst. I just couldn't quite believe it. I'd only known him relish either a good Riesling, sparkling wine or, better yet, a really good Islay Scotch. After a morning of mooching around Darwin doing the tourist thing, we found an Irish pub down by the redeveloped wharf and, as we were hot and thirsty, long, cold drinks were definitely called for. And yes, I have a photograph of Stephen sinking a schooner of beer and thoroughly enjoying it. He took a photograph of me drinking a glass of cider – I just don't like the smell and taste of beer.

After that, we went on a guided tour around Darwin. I hadn't really taken it in that Darwin is geographically the place travellers coming from the north are most likely to arrive at. Many years ago it was the Macassars from the East Indies who appear to have first traded with the Aboriginal people. Darwin was the target of the Japanese bombers in February 1942. They wanted a strategic foothold in Australia after bombing Pearl Harbor. I had no idea how much had happened, how precarious was the defence of this country.

Cyclones too find this area the first land mass as they travel eastwards over the ocean. Cyclone Tracy was testament to the ferocity of such visitors. I didn't know that cyclones build up over the sea and then, when over land, lose momentum and, after blowing everything in their path out of the way, they tamely evaporate. There was very little of Darwin left standing after Tracy came calling on the night of Christmas 1976.

We were taken to a museum that provided a lot of information about the horrors of the bombing and the cyclone. Darwin seems to identify itself a lot with these two events. I didn't see any mention of what happened to the Aboriginal people during these times.

The museum also introduced me to the mind-boggling plight of some of the boat people who found their way to the safe shores of Australia. There were half a dozen dilapidated wooden craft that would have been unsafe in a sheltered bay or quiet river, yet they had brought refugees across the high seas. Whatever were they fleeing from that they would risk the lives of men, women and children in such a way? A desperation in a class of its own. And these days when they arrive here, probably more dead than alive in some cases, we lock them up. This is like the uranium mining and the horrendous treatment of Aboriginals: my mind doesn't know how to grasp the edges.

I knew that swimming in Darwin Harbour was not an option because of the saltwater crocodiles, but I wanted to at least paddle my feet. Stephen gently explained that this was not a good idea because of sea wasps. What are they? Box jellyfish with very, very long tentacles, and being stung can prove fatal! Well, that was that.

For our last evening in Darwin, we bought barramundi and chips and took them to the parklands outside the hotel and watched the sunset. It held all the vividness of a tropical sunset I had imagined and hoped for.

There was a group of Aboriginal people sitting on the grass drinking. I was still apprehensive. A better understanding of why they might find solace in drink didn't overcome my old fear of the unpredictable behaviour of anyone who is drunk. When the police pulled up, I heard one voice crying out, 'I am —. This is my land.' I didn't catch the tribal name. But even if this was his traditional land, what could he do? He wasn't going to be allowed to live there the way his ancestors would have done – even if he knew how. Some people talk with disgust and horror of the Stolen Generations who were taken from their families with the idea of training them to live in white man's society. But what of these lost souls? There will be no peace for them in this lifetime.

The horrible irony was that nearby a group of white fitness fanatics were jumping up and down doing their thing. No one seemed to have complained about them and wanted them moved on. Well, Stephen and I did, actually, but it would have been a pointless exercise trying to get that to happen.

What a puzzle of contradictions was this Northern Territory.

Our last morning in Darwin, and we were waiting for the coach that would take us out to East Arm, where the Ghan train was waiting for us. I was a bit apprehensive. I had been on the Overland to Melbourne but that was a twelve-hour journey during the day. This part of our journey was going to take three days and two nights. Now I was going to experience going from one end of the country to the other – three thousand kilometres.

The Ghan had thirty-two coaches and in total the train measured about 780 metres in length. It was very hard to comprehend. At one point in our journey we'd go round a bend and I'd see the locomotive when I looked left and the end of the last coach when I turned right!

Our cabin was lovely. Not swish posh but the seat was comfortable and we had our own en suite; how funny we can be about privacy. I'd stepped into a completely different world from anything I'd known. All our meals and drinks were included in our fare, which made it all seem the more extravagant.

When we left the cabin to go for our evening meal, we hung a sign on the door and elves came in and made up the bunk beds. Stephen – ever gallant – claimed the top one. A little admission here: I've been known to fall out of bed on a number of occasions at home and he wasn't taking any chances that I'd roll out of the top bunk. It would have been a messy business.

In the mornings when we went to the dining car for breakfast, we hung the sign up again and the elves came in and made up the beds, restoring it to a railway compartment, and provided fresh towels. How good is that!

As soon as we stepped into the lounge car, I thought I'd been transferred to the Orient Express. Wood-panelled walls, old-fashioned sidelights, leather couches along one side with tables; sets of two chairs and a small table between on the other. These chairs became our favourite place to relax and drink sparkling wine before lunch and dinner. Such a tough job!

The dining car. Wow covers it quite neatly, I think. Glass panels separated the tables, each set for four people. White tablecloths, heavy cutlery and crockery. For us, different eating companions each meal. Such delicious meals too. I really don't know how to explain this luxury – on a train, travelling across the middle of Australia.

Stephen's reaction was a surprise for me. A man of modest tastes,

I was delighted to see him relax and settle down to enjoy this luxury. It seems in his bag of special things to be savoured is eating on trains. As I said earlier, Stephen and his young son came to Australia in 1979 and before settling at Daly River they did a two-week tour round Australia. They arrived at Perth, took the Indian Pacific train across to Sydney, the Spirit of Progress from Sydney to Melbourne, the Overland from Melbourne to Adelaide, the old Ghan from Adelaide to Alice Springs and a bus from Alice Springs to Darwin. Although Stephen had driven from Daly River down to Adelaide and back several times, this was the first time he had been on the new Ghan. Imagine, the section from Darwin to Alice Springs has only been open for barely ten years!

Our first whistle-stop was at Katherine and we were booked to go on a cruise along the gorge. Stephen hadn't been to Kakadu before but he and his son had been here. Memories came bubbling to the surface.

The sandstone cliffs of the gorge are rich orange/red and with wonderful curves along their faces showing different layers of rock like a child draws the sea. The same vertical cracks appeared as in the main escarpment between Kakadu and Arnhem Land with slender trees growing in them. We could see these narrow gorges on either side of the main river so all the while we were aware of the criss-cross pattern.

There were painted figures high up the rock face. I wondered how the painters reached that far – maybe it was the Mimi spirits. Stephen recalled taking a photograph of his son looking at them.

We were both somewhat distracted. There was so much majesty around us. We were floating along a gorge made by the Rainbow Serpent. How could those stories of the Creation Ancestors be disregarded? Yet there were those in the party who were untouched and only wanted to hear the sound of their own voices. Perhaps this is what happens when we're faced with our insignificance.

Once again we were made aware of the importance of water. Our guide told us that the day before he couldn't take the boat as far along the gorge because the water was too shallow at one point. The rain that was shadowing our journey had made it possible for us to travel deep into the timelessness of this place. Once again we felt we were being watched over by the gods or the spirits of this land.

As we sat in the lounge car that first afternoon, some of the enormousness of the whole decision to come to Australia and the places he had been, things he had done in those first years, overwhelmed Stephen. He is a man of very deep emotions that he's reluctant to put into words.

Back in the solitude of our cabin, I watched the world go past. I was surprised that the lovely soft savanna woodland reached so far south. Gradually, the trees grew smaller and were replaced by saltbush. Not the empty desert I had anticipated. This was life lusting after life in any way it possibly could.

I pondered about sitting in the train. It was like a caterpillar slowly crawling across the land. No, that wasn't right. It was like a snake. The Rainbow Serpent! And this vast land suddenly became my garden. We were winding our way along a path that would take us from the top end to where we live at the bottom.

Spiritually I would no longer need the safety of the walled garden. I will go on loving it, tending it and thoroughly enjoying the seclusion from other people, but now it's part of a larger garden. I felt as if I'd been liberated from some invisible bondage.

Overnight, while we tried to sleep in our strange moving surroundings, the train had been covering hundreds of kilometres. I woke at about five and watched the sun rise over a vast, flat expanse of red earth, dotted with bushes. How could that be? Not a sign of humans anywhere, except the railway track.

The MacDonnell Ranges appeared on the horizon. We were approaching our last stop – Alice Springs, right in the middle of Australia! Stating the bleeding obvious, some would say, but I was still having trouble getting my head around the simple fact that I was here.

I sometimes think Stephen and I must be part-birds. If there is a chance of a small plane or helicopter ride, we are there at the front of the line. I hadn't realised we'd have the chance of a helicopter ride over Alice Springs and the MacDonnell Ranges.

This country is so different to Kakadu. There's a sense of nothingness. I don't mean there was no vegetation below us; there was. There were river beds too, though the Todd River's more famous for not having water in it.

Our pilot gave us a little information about Pine Gap that we could see in the distance but said nothing at all about the Aboriginal people of the area. It was as if they didn't exist, which I know is not so. The part-Aboriginal mother of my two grandsons came from Alice Springs and continues to live there.

When describing this place, the words forbidding, unforgiving and uncompromising come to my mind. Yet I know that these attributes can be applied to cities and suburbs teeming with people, cars, tall buildings… No, this choice of descriptive words is borne out of the silence, the stillness and the vast horizons. It would take a very special kind of person to be at home in this place, and that is borne out by my son, who loved it when he lived here for a while. He was right about something else: I was in awe of the mountains. I loved their stark severity.

The clouds over Darwin had been fabulous, great billowing creations, a mixture of dark menacing hearts and silver edges. They seemed somehow to keep the heavens contained. If I've wearied at times of the seemingly wide skies outside my studio window, now I know better. Something else that has been changed in me forever. I have always concentrated on the dimensions of the land. What of the spectacle that is the sky over this land? All I could wish for is to have the chance to see it at night with all those stars shining. It's the stars that stop us disappearing altogether into infinity. Small wonder they're often described to children as beloved ones who have died.

The atmosphere on the train was different when we climbed back on board. There'd be no more stops now till we reached Adelaide in about twenty-four hours. I sensed, as we sat in the lounge car, that there were those who were relieved the sightseeing was over and they could just relax and chat. Perhaps they were seasoned travellers and their sense of wonder had diminished or become jaded.

Not all were like that. For our last dinner, we shared our table with a quiet couple. A bit older than us, they carefully told us of some of the people who were important to them, and some of their experiences. We told them a little about us. Somewhere in the conversation was mentioned the importance of writing personal history down to leave as a legacy to the next generations. It was the gods and spirits again.

We saw Jeryl in the corridor the next morning and she told us her husband Norman had mesothelioma. Stephen gave her his business card and we hoped they would send us the memoir Norman had written. It's fundamental to Stephen to open doors of opportunity. Norman may not have long to live, but his story would go on in the written word to influence others if Stephen were given the chance to publish his memoir.

The train trundled inexorably along. We were so thankful we had these long hours to rest and reflect. We pondered over life-changing decisions we had both made to come to Australia and to maintain the ongoing quality of our lives here. We thought of the children and grandchildren who strengthen our links to this country.

There was much to muse on about our journey over the last few days. The wonders we had seen. The people we had met. The chance meetings and discoveries which were not chance at all but were meant to be. New knowledge and affirmations.

The Ghan slowly completed its trek and pulled in sedately at the station in the Adelaide Parklands. It didn't take long before all of the two hundred odd passengers had dispersed – never, most of us, to meet again.

Vigilance

It wasn't till I had a long chat with Annette, my friend of more than twenty years, that I realised I've been walking on a shaky foot suspension bridge over an abyss since I left Forty Green.

Being a child of the universe sounds impressive but it's a lonely way of living, having no one to share life with. Sharing a garden, whether a small one beside a tidal reach with Stephen or one as big as Australia with millions of other people, gives me a sense of belonging. Being a child of the universe now has a sense of perspective.

As any gardener will tell you, it takes constant vigilance to keep a garden beautiful and fruitful. The jabiru, the symbol of vigilance, wasn't a chance meeting either. I did some more reading about this unusual-looking bird in the *Animal Dreaming* book. Yet another gift. The jabiru and I share the same spirit.

Will I ever be the same again? No. This journey was for me a watershed. I don't know what will happen next. I do know there's a Rainbow Serpent in my garden – or is it that I've found a place in the Rainbow Serpent's garden?

Eastwards

Introduction

I started out with excitement and anticipation at this opportunity to discover more of my extended garden that most people call Australia. We had a book launch to go to in Canberra and another in Bermagui on the south coast of New South Wales. For years I had heard many less than complimentary things said about the Hay plains and now I was going to find out what all the fuss was about. With my blissful ignorance of geography, I casually said to Stephen, 'We could go down to Bairnsdale to see Bill and Kay and come back in a sort of big circle.' I ignored his gulp before he agreed. All in all, Stephen drove us 3,200 kilometres in nine days. Halfway through, we learned of the death of our dear friend and my fellow Ginninderra Press writer, Ken Vincent. It wasn't unexpected but it still shocked us badly.

Looking back, I was stunned by the lack of presence of Aboriginal people. Just as they weren't mentioned in Darwin during the bombing or Cyclone Tracy, so, in the places we visited on this journey, there appeared to be no record of them apart from a few place names. How can this be? We travelled through beautiful fertile land with plenty of waterways; surely there must have been tribes all through here at some time? Have we really obliterated them so thoroughly? Stephen reminded me that the absence of physical signs is the effect of their having walked lightly across the land.

We were to visit places I had been before at some time or another and I found memories of all kinds adding extra meaning to this journey. I was disturbed to discover that I have great gaps in my memory too and I believe this is where Mother Nature has stepped in to protect me from life's traumas. I can't re-write the past, but I can add the pleasure of new experiences to the old ones. I have included some of the old memories, otherwise this would have been just a travelogue and our trip meant far more than that.

Adelaide–Hay

Five-thirty a.m. The clock was set for six but I woke early as usual. Outside was so still, with a full moon surprisingly high in the sky. I checked emails and turned the computer off. I love doing that. Stephen made us a cooked breakfast. The sky was adrift with pink clouds as we finished packing, loading the car and doing last-minute tidying up. We left at 7.30.

It sounds feeble to say I hadn't realised quite how far we would be going. I was aware, though, that on this first day Stephen was going to be driving about seven hundred kilometres. I hasten to add that I offered to share the driving. I have a licence and new glasses but he can be very selfish about some things and likes to do all the driving!

The day was full of surprises. We drove through the Barker Inlet wetlands; nothing strange about that as such, except that the traffic built up quickly and, by the time we turned onto the Port Wakefield Road, the traffic was backed up for miles. (We found out when we returned that a bad accident had caused the congestion. I am glad I didn't know that when we were passing; it would have spoiled my enjoyment of driving to explore my vast garden.)

I love living in South Australia, mostly because of its slow pace, but towards the end of a long summer the rolling hills lose much of their appeal and the drive to Truro was quite dreary; the most enthralling part was the sunlight filtering through the clouds. But after Truro we came over the top of the hills and the plain stretched for miles before us. That view hasn't lost its charm over the years but I looked at it through different eyes. I could sense the distance without fear now, and beyond the horizon lay Australia with all its diversity, colour and enchantment.

Stephen did a little detour to drive beside Lake Bonney. As ever, it was tranquil and calm. There are so many good memories attached to this place.

When my family was young, we rented a cabin for a weekend. Somewhere there is a beloved photograph of a man with his three young sons aged ten, nine and six trailing behind him, walking along the waterline of the lake carrying their fishing rods over their shoulders. It was evening and they were all tired. With our youngest son, who was a few months old, I was waiting at the cabin for their return.

Years ago, I went to Lake Bonney with Annette. I don't remember much of that journey with her, but we stopped at the lake at sunset and she took some beautiful photographs, one used as the cover for my first book, *The Silver Cord*, and another of me used in a calendar that was created as a fund-raising project at her workplace. I was Ms February. There were a couple of pelicans floating like galleons and we saw fish leaping to catch mosquitoes. I remember feeling utterly at peace when she took that picture. Then we went on to Renmark; I remember the statues of some lions and unusual water features.

Some years later and a week after I bought my new car, Pegasus the Accent, I went to the Berri Centrelink office for a week to help them catch up on a backlog of work. I stayed at a small motel alone. After work each day, I drove quickly to Lake Bonney to watch the sun setting on the far side of the lake. I even managed to get lost in the back streets of Barmera. There was no street lighting, it was very dark and I had no idea where I was. I drove around hopefully, turned a corner and I was on the main street. I had been quite scared. One evening I drove right round the lake, and the sky and the water were deep crimson. Later, I painted a picture from memory; I still have it.

Just over three years ago, soon after his surgery, Stephen and I stayed in the Barmera Hotel for a night. The lake was pretty much the same. Big gum trees, some dead and stranded in the water, and the far side of the lake hazy as if the tree tops were floating…

We bypassed Barmera this time but stopped in Renmark for morning coffee in a pleasant spot overlooking the river. We were keen to get on and didn't linger.

I had been disappointed by the countryside we had been driving through. All the way from Gawler to Barmera there just seemed to be acres of grey, dead grasses and the bushes were scrubby with harsh grey wood and a thatch of dull green leaves. It had not been inspiring but I did get a lovely surprise after Renmark. It was almost as if someone had driven along sprinkling a packet of sunflower seeds. Every now and then we passed a patch of them – not the big dinner-plate-sized ones; these were smaller and delicate with several flower heads on each stem, but they were the same golden colour and made me smile.

We drove on to Mildura, passing through the top corner of Victoria. It was lovely here and I remembered the wide, tree-lined streets.

I went to Mildura shortly after my son died. I recall the gaol in nearby Wentworth. I was overwhelmed by the sense of desolation and violence. A better memory was the deep impression that was made on me by the sight of the Murray and Darling rivers converging. (I wrote about that in *Tales From My Patagonia*.) I started going along the road to Broken Hill but after a hundred kilometres or so felt too afraid to continue. Also, my travelling companion was an insulin-dependent diabetic and not prepared for this extra adventure. I have always been rather sorry I didn't go as far as Broken Hill. Perhaps there will be another time. I remember there seemed to be so many dead trees beside the road and I was amazed by the deep red of the soil and brought a small amount home. I have it still in a bottle with three other different colour sands I collected from Victor Harbor, Semaphore and Goolwa. The only other thing I remember was driving back to Renmark and the fruit fly quarantine station.

After Mildura, we were in New South Wales. We pulled in at Gol Gol to have our picnic lunch by the river but it was only a brief stop. The river Murray was as beautiful and distinctive as ever. We were joined by a Murray magpie that looked just like Scruffy, the untidy Murray magpie who used to feed out of our hands at home; this one even had a sore foot like Scruffy.

The road to Hay. This was it. The long stretch of nothing. Except it wasn't like that. The Hay plains were vast but had a softness that was so gentle on my senses. They were covered in small bushes with pale green leaves which gave the look of a constantly moving ocean. There were solitary, slender trees, or now and then a huddle in the distance, but no enormous old gums. We watched the same unusual-shaped clouds for miles and miles.

We saw about a dozen emus. I didn't know they travelled in flocks. They reminded me of very large chickens and I was glad there was a fence to keep them off the road (though they are capable of jumping over). Were they hawks or eagles we saw? One swooped and dived for lunch.

I could see why people say the Hay plains are deadly dull. The road was straight. It was quite exciting to go round the very occasional bend, except why were the bends there anyway? There were a few gentle rises but really it was quite flat.

More important for me, on reflection, I could feel a connection between the savanna woodland in Kakadu and the rounded bushes of the Hay plains. Both so vast and unspoiled by people and both still filled with hidden life and rich beauty. Is it this reminder of our insignificance that makes people shun such places?

On the outskirts of Hay, we stopped at the Shearers' Hall of Fame. Such a hoot. I bought some tiny ugg boots for Bertie. (Bertie was, at the time of writing, the unborn child of my youngest son, David, who laughed when I gave them to him, even though it would be the following winter before Hamish, as he is really called, could wear them.) I also found a tea towel printed with the words of a shearers' contract from a hundred years ago for Steve, my brother in Dorset, who likes the task of shearing his sheep. A bit later, in the town of Hay, we found some lovely black and white postcards of the shearers of old and their enormous sheds; I sent them to him too. (I had a chuckle when Steve wrote to thank me. He was comparing a flock of forty-five thousand to his two hundred. Just one of those small insights into the differences between the places we live.)

I fell in love with a beautiful leather purse that Stephen bought for me in the Shearers' Hall of Fame. It is soft and looks and feels as if I have had it for years. It is the same deep red as the one Mother gave me in 1996 and I experienced pure nostalgia as I transferred the piece of string from that purse into the new one. (For those who aren't aware of the tradition, when giving a new purse, it is supposed to have inside a silver coin and a piece of string for luck.)

Our motel room was much like so many we have stayed in, simple and comfortable. We went for a walk in the warm sun before dinner and found the Hay railway station – Stephen's idea of heaven, though even I could see it was lovely following its restoration about ten years previously.

Hay–Canberra

Sleep was elusive till long after midnight. I could hear the distant sound of trucks going along the highway but that wasn't what kept me awake. I felt the presence of an old Aboriginal woman in the room. There was a gentle insistence till I accepted her embrace from one wise woman to another. This was the first time I had felt this and I am certain it is linked to my experiences in the Northern Territory. Can it be that I have a spirit family here in this land I call my garden? And will they make themselves known to me if I am careful – respectful? I hope that this is so, not me trying to make it so. It has strengthened the feeling that I belong here.

By eight, we were ready to leave. Before we crossed the bridge and left town, we drove down by the Murrumbidgee river. With the early morning sunlight sparkling through giant gum trees, it was exquisitely tranquil and a beautiful start to our day. I could almost hear the echoing voices from the past, children playing, splashing in the river, families gathered around a campfire cooking the game hunted from the vast surrounding plains. Surely this was an ideal place to sing and tell stories of their Dreamtime?

The Hay plains as such had ended at Hay. For the rest of our journey till Wagga Wagga, the Murrumbidgee would be winding beside the road to our left, apparent only by the trees that kept it company. They had that same hazy quality as the trees at Lake Bonney and seemed somehow to be floating. On our right, paddocks stretched. We saw lots of sheep and cows, and fields of some crop we couldn't identify.

We pulled in at Narrandera for morning coffee. I was surprised how quickly the traffic built up at some roadworks, because we seemed to have seen very little traffic on the move. Narrandera had recently celebrated one hundred and fifty years. It is a sedate town built on a gentle hillside. I couldn't find postcards anywhere. Odd! As it turned out, this was something I had trouble with everywhere we went.

We sighted our first hills before Wagga Wagga, a sort of teasing for what was to come with the Brindabella mountains that provide a backdrop to Canberra. Wagga Wagga reminded me of Warrnambool, with its wide main highway and lots of industrial buildings either side, and of course the presence of the military.

We felt no need to go and explore the town or its shops, so continued to Gundagai. I had come here with Annette years ago and I couldn't see the long trestle railway bridge that I thought I remembered. All that was left was a wooden bridge over the old highway. Stephen told me the stretch of highway we drove on was quite recently upgraded, which has probably added to my confusion. Having said that, the area we sat in to have lunch beside the Dog on the Tucker Box, away from the large petrol station and associated cafés, was lovely and peaceful, and set us up nicely for the trek to Yass.

More and more we were among the hills and then the Brindabella mountains that were twenty shades of blue and grey in the distance. They appeared majestic and patient as if waiting for my return. They are part of my extended garden, and perhaps this is why I feel so connected to them. I wonder if the old ones who lived here once felt something similar. Part of me wishes I had lived here in another time, when I could have enjoyed these places without the clutter of modern times, when affinity with the landscape was just accepted.

The hills began to turn a richer green and the leaves on the trees beside the road were vivid.

I have always loved Canberra. It is something to do with the mountains and the fact that the only people I have been here with are Annette and Stephen – there are no traumatic memories. Instead, as we drove through Canberra I was trying to remember places, but nothing seemed familiar. This was partly due to there being so many roadworks and countless new apartment blocks going up. We never did find out who was going to be living in them.

I could see a plume of smoke and smelt the unique fragrance of a bushfire. No doubt some Canberrans, remembering the fires of 2003, would have been anxious.

The hotel in Dickson was much as I remembered it from our visit in 2012. We went for a stroll before we had dinner at the nearby Vietnamese restaurant. Stephen loves this food but we haven't found a restaurant in Adelaide that he likes as well as this particular place.

It was an early night for us. We had covered a lot of miles but Stephen didn't seem to be affected at all, for which I was thankful.

Canberra

I certainly slept better last night, which was a relief. Today our first adventure was to go to Mount Ainslie and as usual we started out early. Mount Ainslie has stunning panoramic views of Canberra and the surrounding mountains and of course Black Mountain and the unmistakable Telstra Tower.

Over twenty years ago on my first trip to Canberra, I was travelling alone by bus from Melbourne. I can still remember so clearly the frisson of excitement and fear when a white spire kept appearing as the road wound through the hills. I thought it was a visitor from outer space. I also remember the friends that had met me off the bus laughing when I told them and then later took me to the lookout at the top and I saw Canberra spread before me, a magical network of lights beneath a start-studded sky.

Stephen and I looked straight down War Memorial Drive to Parliament House. Stephen took photos of some crimson rosellas and I saw a very shy female fairy wren. There were lots of crows up there, scuffling in the bark like the blackbirds do. I have never seen that before. The air was fresh and clean. A fabulous way to start the day. The lookout is designed so you can look far with a 360-degree range. There is a sense of timelessness that even the buildings and roads do not intrude upon.

We have an extraordinary capital city. It comes in for lots of rude comments but more because of the antics of politicians than the actual city. I love coming here again and again.

We meandered round to Manuka. I remember having coffee here with Bill Tully and Ian and Mary McFarlane two or three years ago. It is still the place to be seen to have coffee and gossip. A nice enough atmosphere with the big trees; just a bit pretentious, I suppose, but, when I think about it, most of these places are these days. We have become a nation of posing coffee drinkers.

Manuka's Paperchain bookshop has a lovely atmosphere. I found a small edition of Tolkien's *Farmer Giles of Ham*, a story with dragons and so on. He apparently wrote it after the *Hobbit* and before the *Lord of the Rings*. I also found a Landmark edition of the works of Xenophon – another book to enhance my studies of Ancient Greece. Stephen bought a couple of books and could have bought more. Always the sign of a good bookshop.

We were meeting Kevin and Barbara Olds for lunch at a café adjoining the Glassworks Gallery but as we were early we went for a walk around the lake. Even with the new apartments, it is still very peaceful-looking along the lake and certainly didn't feel as if we were in the centre of a city.

We did the tourist thing around the gallery and watched a young woman making a glass dish. It was fascinating to see her working with what started being a blob of bright orange molten glass attached to the end of a long rod. She had to keep this hot by returning it to the furnace every few minutes and in between sat on a special chair with arms and she rolled the rod along the arms and also blew gently through the rod until the blob eventually became an incredibly beautiful shallow dish. I know nothing of this art but was astounded when she took a blowtorch to the edges of her dish before detaching it from the rod.

We had a look around the gift shop and the display area. Lovely things but cost-prohibitive. Stephen fell in love with a piece on display. It cost just over $5,000. A dish like the one we had watched being made was hundreds of dollars.

We met Kevin and Barbara in the café, which specialised in burgers. I have never much liked burgers, except very occasionally a Junior Whopper from Hungry Jacks. Here, the menu was extraordinary, with such variety. One thing in common, though: they were all large and dripped their sauces. Barbara was understandably full of her launch that evening. It is always so exciting and nerve-racking. We made sure we knew where the launch venue was and set off for an afternoon of exploring.

We drove to the recently opened National Arboretum. Annette had shown me photographs but I was still flabbergasted to see it. It is part of the plan for remediation of the areas of pine forest that were destroyed in the January 2003 fires. There are two buildings settled in the hillside. The larger one was staggering; it had the same line on its roof as the hills behind it. Inside, it was enormous with high vaulted ceilings and gigantic wooden beams. It holds a large information section, a shop, a café and to one end a bonsai display area.

The bonsai display was enchanting but I felt conflicting emotions. The little trees were things of great beauty yet I deplored the fact that they were, some of them, as old as me and yet were so stunted. What a life. Annette later reminded me that the craftsmen often use the new shoots that come up when a tree has been destroyed. Mostly they will be mown down or lost in some way. Becoming bonsai trees gives them a new life. I guess I can go with that.

We looked around the gift shop and we had a cup of tea, just so we could enjoy the building and the fantastic view across Lake Burley Griffin. It was a perfect day for it. Not too hot, and the sky was filled with billowing clouds. Outside, the children's playground was superb. The equipment looked like the giant gum nuts in the books of May Gibbs.

Another piece of artwork was mind-blowing. It was made up of old iron tools and bits of machinery built into an enormous eagle's nest with an eagle standing on the edge also made up of bits and pieces. I love this kind of clever installation artwork.

The arboretum is testimony to man's imagination and ability to look into the future. In ten and twenty years' time, this will be a wonderland. Areas of trees with different-coloured leaves and shapes from all over the world – 'Wow' comes to mind!

All the while this day I was conscious of the Telstra tower. It made me smile each time it appeared like a watch dog. Again and again I was reminded of my first impression of it and smiled to myself. We solved the mystery of the smoke; they were doing a controlled burn on the slopes of Black Mountain. It looked really eerie and, depending on the wind, sent the delicious smell of bushfire smoke across the city.

I have never seen Canberra look so lovely as it did today. Is it part of the magic of knowing this is all part of my garden? I don't know. I do know I felt that wonderful sense of belonging again.

It was too early to go to the venue for Barbara's book launch so we decided to pop into Belconnen shopping centre. In all my trips to Canberra, I still don't remember which shopping precinct is which. It really was good that Stephen was driving otherwise we would have been going round and round in circles – helped of course by the lovely road system with all its roundabouts. Thanks to the centre's Dick Smith store, I now have an updated laptop for when we go away on trips. Lucky me!

We arrived at the art gallery where the launch was to be. We followed the directions we had been given and found ourselves driving to the edge of suburbia and down a dirt road. Set in a rural area, an old homestead has become public property and the main house and the attached assortment of shearing sheds and so on have been converted to studios where workshops are held. It was lovely, particularly in the evening light.

There was a display called Paper Road, which showcased unusual uses of handmade paper. I have tried to make paper and it isn't as easy as I thought it would be.

The launch was lively. Several people remembered Stephen from when he lived in Canberra. I was moved and surprised that Barbara told everyone it was at the launch of *Facing Cancer* in Canberra a couple of years ago when she realised she could put together another collection of her own poetry. Quite a tribute, I thought.

But the launch did have its little drama. Stephen carefully set up the books for sale and went to open the cash box for the PayPal card reader gizmo and no key! He searched everywhere and could only conclude that it had fallen out of his pocket during the day. He knew he had brought it with us because he kept feeling it to reassure himself that it was in his pocket. Kevin showed remarkable resourcefulness by locating a small crowbar from his car and literally jimmied the box open. Poor Stephen was quite shaken up by this.

On the way back to our motel, we decided to just grab a bottle of wine and some nibbles for supper. Once in the room, Stephen checked his emails. There was one from Maureen. She had gone to see Ken at the hospital and he was in a coma. We learned later that Ken's last words to his son were, 'F— Tony Abbott.' I wish I had known that then so I could have laughed as we did when we heard about it. Instead I felt lost and sad.

Canberra–Bermagui

Some days have things in them that reduce us to helpless laughter, and we just enjoyed one of those moments this afternoon, but I will come back to that. For now, I will say that it is about four p.m. We are on the balcony of our hotel suite drinking champagne overlooking Bermagui Bay. It is cloudy but not cold. Mount Gulaga overlooks the bay and is stunning, and there are lots of Harley Davidson motorbikes outside!

Our day got off to a slightly different start. No breakfast in the hotel room today. I really wanted to have a cooked breakfast beside Lake Ginninderra at the Ha Ha Café as we did on our last visit. Good job we had called in there on the way home last night and booked a table, as it was quite busy and we had the last outside table.

Eggs benedict with bacon and coffee was delicious. It is such a lovely setting there with the lake and the big trees around it. The Saturday morning crowd seemed a lively lot too. There were half a dozen galahs in a tree, looking so picturesque chortling to each other.

It had rained heavily during the night, but the burn-off was still smoking. There were also great wreaths of mist, which Stephen told me was rising off the Murrumbidgee. It was ethereal. Canberra certainly turned on her best weather for us. We left Lake Ginninderra at about nine-thirty and set off for Cooma. I finally saw a mob of kangaroos in a paddock. Not quite in the heart of Canberra as I have seen them before, but at least they weren't roadkill. We ran in tandem with a disused railway track for miles. It was reminiscent of a bygone era.

I was surprised how green the hills were outside Canberra. It was very peaceful and rural and somehow so typical of Australia that our capital city is nestled in unchanged countryside without the suburban sprawl of Sydney or Melbourne and embraced by the circle of mountains.

Cooma is quite unusual. This is the gateway to the High Country. The main street is on a hill and there was a humming atmosphere. The air was much cooler too. I managed to buy some postcards to send, but there was not much of a choice. As we were waiting to pay for the cards, I overheard a conversation. It seems you need permits – even the locals – to go out to the Kosciuszko National Park for camping and fishing. A flood of good memories again.

I remember so clearly when Peter and Annette took me to the High Country to see the snow. It had been thirty-odd years since I had last seen snow in England. We stopped at Cooma then – it must have been to get permits – and I remember something being said about putting chains on the tyres. I can still see it vividly. We drove round a bend and there in the distance was a range of very large mountains with real snow on their tops. (I seem to remember we passed near Thredbo, where the disastrous landslide occurred in 1997.)

It got better and better. We drove through the snow-covered country and I saw my first snow gums. The colours of the bark were unbelievable. In my mind, gum trees are synonymous with heat yet here they were up to their knees in snow. There was a creek running with small icebergs floating on it. I was in a fairyland.

The air was still and cold. I collected snow on my hand and it felt the same. I saw the sun glitter on it the same. I tasted it. It was the same as I remembered from my childhood. It wasn't long till my socks and sandals were soaking and my feet cold. I looked up the side of a towering mountain that was white and unsullied by any sign of people. The sky was brilliant blue.

With me still bemused, we left the snow country and drove around by Lake Jindabyne before heading back to Canberra. We drove along a dirt road through a lush green valley with a wandering creek. We came up into the pine forests that towered over us all the way home. All along the valley and in among the pine trees were slender acacia trees covered in yellow blossom – the clusters of little balls that look wonderful and smell horrible, or perhaps it is an acquired taste.

I remember too that all those pine trees were among the ones destroyed in the January 2003 fires. The landscape has changed beyond recognition. I hope I never forget that day in the snow and the wonderful log fire I sat beside when we arrived home...

Stephen and I went into a bookshop and he bought me a map of Tolkien country that the author created before he wrote the *Lord of the Rings*. Tolkien seems to be travelling with me this trip.

Somewhere after we left Cooma and passed through Nimmitabel, Stephen said, 'Look out of the back window.' There, looking very large and brooding, was Mount Kosciuszko.

Out of Nimmitabel we seemed to be climbing higher and higher and I felt we were driving over the top of the world. It wasn't exactly menacing; Stephen suggested hostile. It silenced words. The rolling hills were colourless, covered in rocky outcrops as if the rocks were impatient with being underground. No gentle green here. But there weren't just rolling hills, there were conical shape ones with sharp pointed tops. Perhaps it was the clouds too. They were enormous. Some had silver lacy edges, others inky hearts. Very brooding. It was as if the earth was reaching up to them.

Eventually we came to the forests. The trees were magnificent. What a tree fix! We stopped at Pipers Point at the top of Brown Mountain. Another place I had been with Annette.

We came up from Bega and we literally drove up into the mist. Annette could barely see beyond the bonnet of the car. An enormous logging truck came down the steep road that we were going up. At the top, we stopped to look at the view, but it wasn't there! I do have photos of the beautiful trees and a robin. It was eerie up there and I loved it, even though it was very cold.

The trees at Pipers Point are awesome. Another silencing time. Stephen and I watched the sun chasing clouds across the landscape far below. There is a little path that wanders in a circle up and down steps that gave us a wonderful opportunity to view the incredibly high trees and the lichens on the rocks. Stephen had been to the lookout before but not walked along this little path. I love being able to show him new places.

We slowly came down the steep, winding mountain road. Hard reality waited for us at a sharp bend. Police cars and motorbikes. The bikers standing around looked shocked. One of their group had dropped his bike. We followed the ambulance down. At the bottom of the mountain, the ambulance pulled in. It had been going very slowly. Hard not to read stuff into that. (I see outside our balcony the orange motorbike that was part of the group of riders at the scene of the accident.)

Down and away from the mountains everything was lushly green, very much dairy country – hence the cheese factory at Bega. We didn't go into Bega but turned north to go to Cobargo. We came over the brow of a hill and it was like stepping through a time warp: one main street with old wooden shops on either side. We stopped there and had tea and scones and I wrote all of my postcards, except one for Ella.

There was a strange atmosphere in Cobargo. Perhaps it was just the lowering clouds, the chill dampness. Stephen told me about a good gathering – a *Voice* forum – that Ginninderra Press had in the town's community hall years ago.

It wasn't far to Bermagui, which really is lovely; we could be in Queensland with the palm trees and very picturesque bay. I hope we see it with the sun shining before we leave on Monday morning. Across the bay Mount Gulaga is watching over us. They say it looks like a sleeping woman and I can see that, but it is also called Mount Dromedary because it looks like a camel kneeling down.

We had some difficulty finding the hotel because it stood right beside a motel with almost the same name. How silly! We pulled into a drive-through belonging to the wrong one and a man with a wheezy voice told us where we had to go. After driving through another drive-through bottle shop and up onto a makeshift car park beyond, we gingerly walked back down into the pub/hotel.

The motorbikes? Well, it seems this was the annual fund-raiser in Bermagui for cancer research. The young woman at the reception window at the end of the bar told us the funfair part would be closing at five 5 p.m. and things would be quiet then. Oh, but they were having a live band later on! I must confess to initially being rather shaken by being amid so many large bikers.

The hotel was built in the 1880s and reminds me of the old section of the Largs Hotel near where we live. We have an old-fashioned suite, not a room. One armchair is covered in tapestry material and has a sneaky little place inside the arms where you can put your glass. The bathtub is big enough to swim in and has those spa swirly things. The ceilings are high and it reminds me of a gracious old lady wondering slightly what she is doing at this sedate seaside resort in the company of a lot of mature bikers sporting grey beards and black leather.

As I said, we are sitting on the upstairs balcony sipping sparkling wine. Every now and then, the quiet is shattered by the roar of a motorbike. A live rock and roll band has been playing but has now stopped. Perhaps it was the warm-up for tonight! There are bikers everywhere.

These blokes are, for the most part, large, long-haired and bearded, and there is lots of laughter. I hope they don't get too hammered later and spoil what seems to be a cheerful mood.

I watched three young men walking up and down making comments about the motorbikes parked. I sensed a hunger. Then one donned his helmet and got on one of the motorbikes. He was intending to do a slick U-turn and roar off down the road like the big boys do. Trouble was, he misjudged and dropped the bike, and went rolling down the street. He got up and seemed unhurt – except for his pride. I heard a voice call, 'That was a bit amateurish.' No sympathy there. I watched as the owner picked up his bike and wheeled it ignominiously out of sight – leaving a great patch of oil on the road. A bit later, someone put sand down and I heard him say there had been some expensive damage done to the bike.

It was nice lingering on the balcony reading a book. Then we plucked up our courage and went down and had fish and chips for dinner outside under the veranda. The band played long and loud into the night, although from our suite we could only really hear the drums and the bass guitar.

Bermagui & Tilba Tilba

Stephen is sixty-eight today. Age is a funny thing. We are inclined to measure it in years when we speak about someone, but I think we should be thinking in terms of experience, compassion and wisdom and Stephen has those in abundance.

It is still cloudy this morning so we aren't seeing this place at its best. We have been sitting on the balcony again enjoying our breakfast and a few bikers have turned up for theirs downstairs. Conversation is lively. We even have patches of sunlight which turn the sea to green. We've watched a few fishing boats head off to the wide open sea – this is, after all, essentially a fishing port.

I long for some stillness and silence to think about where we have been on this journey. I have been making notes as we travelled but I need a map to remind myself of place names and so on. The sea is a constant shushing sound both soothing and unsettling. This isn't like the stillness and silence at home; here I am aware of the constant movement of the sea rather than the gentle ebb and flow of water in the tidal reach. Mount Gulaga is both brooding and benevolent and seems to dominate the bay. but not in the same way as Mount Wellington broods over Hobart. There are small fishing boats scuttling out to sea. I ponder about the whereabouts of the spirits of this place. How they must revere this paradise of sunshine, surf and mountains.

An email from Rachel told us Ken had died. Peacefully in his sleep on Saturday just after midnight. It is what I wanted for him but initially I just didn't know how to respond to the news. It wasn't like when my son died. Maybe Ken is with Audrey Hepburn, as he wrote about in the book I launched for him, *The Day I Didn't Die*. Except he did die. I will miss him at book launches – and I shall miss our lively lunches. He has been for me, and many other writers, such a source of quiet strength and encouragement

Stephen and I had arranged to have morning coffee with Ian and

Mary at their house on Sunday morning. The drive along the coast was superb and we found their house at Beauty Point without difficulty. What a wonderful setting, and well named (though it was recently renamed Wallaga Lake). While Mary made scones, Ian took us to the edge of 'his' lake to a small pagoda-type lookout. We sat and chatted, with the mountain perfectly reflected in the water behind us. There were many swans and everything was peaceful. Ian was naturally anxious about his launch that afternoon and the speech he was to give. We writers are all the same, it seems.

Back at their house, we had tea and scones on the veranda, and two rainbow lorikeets came and sat on the railing. Another wow moment! A touch ironic too because Ian gave Stephen a birthday card with a picture of the lorikeets inside. I had left a copy of *There's a Rainbow Serpent in My Garden* and Mary started reading it while she was waiting for her scones to cook. Ian read it after we left and before his launch, which was at four o'clock. Gosh.

We left them to go sightseeing. The shock of Ken whooshed in and we went to the Foxglove garden. Stephen brought me here on our last trip to Canberra in early December 2011.

I was enchanted by the big shady trees reaching over winding pathways. We were lucky it was just the right time of year and there were beautiful foxgloves that instantly took me even further back to my English country childhood. There were so many irises; they always make my fingers itch for a paintbrush. In some places ivy covered the ground and I was surprised to see an old garden gate. Well, strictly speaking it wasn't the gate that surprised me, but the fact that there was no garden fence. It simply stood as a solitary guard. Nearby was an equally old garden seat. How inviting it was. I could imagine sitting there reading a book, or writing a letter while enjoying a cup of tea. At one end of the garden, we walked through a long wisteria arch and there was a folly. Two stone walls like the corner of a fallen-down house with ivy covering them, an old stone urn and mossy flagstones. Behind it was a pond covered in water lilies. There was the most wonderful sense of peace here. Somewhere a blackbird was singing. More ramblings and we came to the herb gardens. I love these. I always wanted an old wagon wheel set in the garden with different herbs growing between the spokes. These gardens made such an impact on me; I went home and wrote several poems about things I had seen.

The gardens had been taken over by some new people and weren't as well tended as before, or maybe it was the end of summer and they were doing a lot of renovations. But it was peaceful with lovely birdsong and I could calm down a bit. We took photos of roses and dahlias and some doves in an old-fashioned aviary. The tea shop was closed but not the garden centre. The plants looked so tempting. I wished I could scoop some up and bring them home with us.

We revisited Central Tilba. It seemed hollow and deserted compared with our previous visit. Apparently they have a market on Saturdays and it bustles then. What a pity we missed it. We bought cheese, chutney and marmalade at the cheese factory, our small attempt to support local artisans.

At the top of the hill behind the town, there is of course a lookout. It really is beautiful countryside around there and well worth the climb even though we didn't get to the top. We came back down and had a glass of sparkling wine and shared a spinach pasty at the pub, and I felt better. One last shop and, as a result, I came home with a charcoal grey cardigan made of Peruvian alpaca and a Kashmiri wall hanging/bedspread with a Tree of Life design. I will lay it on the guest bedroom bed.

Next it was on to the Tilba winery for Ian's launch. It was just as I remembered: a lovely dirt track through the trees to the hidden large log cabin that is the winery. We had lunch here under the vine-covered veranda last time.

It was very much Keats and his mellow fruitfulness, and a beautiful place for a book launch. Whatever Ian's misgivings about his speech, he responded marvellously to the atmosphere created by good friends and fellow writers. With some prompting from Stephen and the other guests, Ian read a very moving poem about social injustice which met with resounding applause.

Later, we met Ian and Mary back at Bermagui at a Thai restaurant at the wharf. We sat outside in the quiet evening, no motorbikes, no loud music, just the wind and the sea and gentle conversation. It was with a sense of satisfaction that we returned to our quaint hotel suite.

Bermagui–Bairnsdale

Monday morning it was still warm and overcast. We made our own breakfast, which we had out on the balcony, and made an early start, as it was going to be a long drive down to Bairnsdale to stay with Bill and Kay Cotter.

There were to be a couple of surprises ahead for me today. We began driving through the beautiful countryside of tall trees on steep hillsides sloping down to the sea and went past a sign – 'Kianninny'. I could hardly believe my eyes. I had remembered where Bega was but had no recollection of where Kianninny was. What a flood of lovely memories.

Years ago, Annette drove us over to the east coast. We stayed at Kianninny, a group of log cabins set back among big trees and beside a lake. They had a Hundred Acre Wood theme from the Winnie the Pooh books. We had a log fire because it was very cold and I remember we fed possums under the veranda. It was a magical place and we laughed a lot. We went for a walk among the trees and found lots of wild flowers and fungi. I wonder if I still have the photos. So many have been lost.

We looked at the jetty at Tathra. It seemed familiar; I know now that I had been there with Annette.

And Merimbula with its large bay and marina filled with boats. We browsed in a bookshop, which Stephen said had changed quite a lot; it now had a coffee shop at one end. This does seem to work well. I came out empty-handed but Stephen found a book of poems about trains. He really only bought it because it had the words to the Flanders and Swann song 'A Slow Train'. I checked out a toy shop in the hope of finding an unusual teddy bear for Bertie, but no luck. Merimbula seemed to be a bustling little town and I am sorry that I was still so shocked from the news of Ken that I didn't look at it properly.

Eden isn't very far from Merimbula and I kept getting tantalising views of the mountains beside and behind us as we drove down the coast. I did enjoy our time there. We went up to a lookout where there were yellow-tailed black cockatoos up in the trees. They didn't sound much like cockatoos at all. From there, we went to the Whale Museum. I had no idea whaling was such a large industry in this area in years gone by. It was interesting and horrifying somehow. There was a large old map of Australia on the wall and it showed where the Aborigines went all the way around the country in their fragile canoes. They travelled so far as part of their complicated marriage laws.

We stopped at a café and sat outside and had coffee and shared a delicious Italian-style savoury muffin. We decided to buy some sandwiches for lunch, which we planned to have somewhere along the way. (They turned out to be very, very good.)

As we usually do, we wandered around a gallery/gift shop. It was spacious, with a warm and welcoming atmosphere. I noticed in the window some snakes carved from slender branches and set inside hollow logs. They were quite large and expensive but I did like them. Stephen found paintings by an artist called Sue O'Laughlin. There were several of her pieces but he did that sudden intake of breath in front of a small one with waves like mist pounding against a cliff. So of course it had to come home with us. I left the woman wrapping it as we looked around some more. I found a beautiful small wooden snake and that came home with us too. So much for my vow of not buying mementos.

Stephen pointed out a couple of books by Beryl Gamble on display. He showed me the Ginninderra Press imprint on the spine. Apparently there had been a good launch in Eden some years ago. I love it when we find GP books unexpectedly like that. I told the ladies in the shop about the GP connection and who Stephen was. They could recall the book launch. Stephen waited outside for me. I know he was pleased to find the books but he doesn't like attention being drawn to him.

The day was starting to clear a bit and the sun started shining through the clouds. We headed off to the Ben Boyd tower. Such an extraordinary building, standing twenty-three metres high. It is a square building on the top of a headland and the owner wanted it to be used as a lighthouse but permission was refused and it was only used as a whale-sighting tower. It must have been an amazing feat to bring the rock in from Sydney to build it. It has deep-set windows that reminded me of the lighthouse at Cape Otway, except these blocks were cemented together rather than just set tightly on one another as at the lighthouse.

We walked down some steps carved into the cliff face and we could see fabulous different-coloured strata alongside us. It reminded me of Pirate Bay in Tasmania. The sun cleared the clouds and the water was brilliant aqua with sparkling white foam as the waves smashed onto the rocks below.

It was time to move on; we still had a long drive ahead. The winding road took us inland through wonderful forests. This really did remind me of Tasmania. At some point near the state border, we pulled off the road to a picnic area to enjoy our sandwiches.

Back on the road, we saw a sign for Mallacoota. Bill Cotter had mentioned they had been there earlier this year, so we thought we would go and see. A short way along the side road was another sign, for Gypsy Point. A quick decision to go and see. And what a shock for me. I had been there before. I remembered the picnic tables beside the water, not a river but an inlet. This was where I came with Annette.

Till Bill took us there about four years ago, I had long been mistaken that Annette took me to Lakes Entrance. In fact, Annette and I had a picnic at Gypsy Point before driving back to Kianninny. There were kangaroos hopping about and a couple of boats moored. On the way back to the cabin, we stopped in Merimbula to have dinner. The restaurant we went into had Greek-style murals on the walls. I remember Annette's pleasure being able to show me.

When I mentioned this to Stephen, he knew the restaurant: it was upstairs over the bookshop we had been to. So after all these years I have found it again. How lucky I am.

We resumed our journey down to Mallacoota. What an amazing place. There is a council-owned caravan park that stretches all across the grassed area overlooking a tranquil inlet. It was like a tent city and some people obviously stay there for extended periods of time. There were tents attached to tents so their occupants had more than one 'room'. Some tents even had their own little solar panels. We were quite stunned by it all. I loved the pelicans and fairy wrens and the way the ocean lapped against a sandbar but I'm not sure I would want to stay there with so many people, even in a motel or in a cabin on a caravan park. Bill later told us about another quieter bay nearby, where they had been.

After Mallacoota, the map tells me we headed inland but still following the line of the coast. Endless miles of tall trees. How I love these areas. By the time we reached Cann River, we were ready for a quick coffee. This is where the Cann River Highway meets the Princes Highway. I could see from the map that Stephen had driven us the much longer route by taking the Princes Highway. A bit late perhaps, but I did begin to be concerned that I had asked too much. The road was winding and needed concentration in a way the straight road across the Hay plains didn't.

Orbost shows on the map as a large town. The railway line from Melbourne used to end here but now stops at Bairnsdale. I think we were both touristed out by this time and we didn't go into the town centre.

The trees and the mountains seemed to gradually draw away as the road wound ever further westward. I vaguely knew this area is the southernmost point of the Great Dividing Range. I know that sounds a bit obvious, but it was noticeable as we travelled that there were more paddocks than forest, and the mountains became distant sentinels watching our progress.

I usually have my camera on my lap ready for a quick photograph of passing features of interest but for some reason I didn't just when I needed it. We were going round a long curve and to our right appeared a long old railway trestle bridge. We went beside it for a while, but such was the nature of the road we couldn't stop. I was slightly mesmerised, I think, and didn't try reaching for the camera. Stephen is fascinated by the history of the area, and muttered about the wasted opportunity to keep the trestle in use even as a tourist attraction. The trestle just gracefully curved away and disappeared into the forest. Oh, how I wish I had taken a photograph. I'm certain it would have said far more than words can.

We paused at Lakes Entrance long enough to buy some sparkling wine to have with dinner. I love that I have good memories of this place too. We have been here a couple of times with Bill and Kay and had coffee on a boat moored on the river. I might not like boats much but I did enjoy that. But this was not going to be a time to linger. I think we were both weary of travelling for this day and the setting sun was going to make driving less than pleasant for the last stretch to Bairnsdale. Bill rang and wondered where we were.

It was good to arrive and relax. We would be sleeping in the little A-frame caravan in the garden – our luxury hotel! We were lucky that, while autumn was making itself known, the nights were not too cold, so we slept well.

Bill ordered a pizza for dinner and we settled down to exchange the stuff of our lives, news of family and so on.

Bairnsdale

I woke to the sound of different birdsong and cows lowing in the paddock nearby. So different to waking by the tidal reach with the sounds of dolphins splashing and the trundle of trains across the bridge over the water.

Bill and Kay left just after seven-thirty to go to the campus where Kay is studying part-time for a degree in Fine Arts, so we had the house to ourselves for breakfast and a day mooching around.

We wandered around Bairnsdale and found the bookshop. Under new management, it had a different atmosphere from when we visited last time and it didn't relieve us of any of our money. We set off in search of McLeods Morass, another favourite place. We drove around quite a bit before we found it. It is an odd place really, set to the side of the town. There was a sense of abandonment. The duck-shooting season had started at the weekend. It all seemed so contradictory. A lot of time, energy and money have been spent to create a bird sanctuary, yet, nearby, people were allowed to shoot the ducks at certain times of the year.

We drove down to Paynesville and found a fish and chip shop, took our lunch to a picnic area and watched a pair of black swans. One of them was utterly indifferent and slept, bobbing on the water. The other kept picking up and moving bits of the seaweed stranded on the shore. We thought at first it was building a nest, but we came away utterly bewildered. The silver gulls are like our own, and of course we fed them our leftover chips and singled out the injured one to get most. Maybe it was the time of year, but the same air of weariness shrouded the place.

We decided to just go back to Crooke Street. In the stillness I wrote some poetry and Stephen read Bill's marvellous new collection of poetry, which, like his last one, he has handwritten in calligraphy. We were horrified to discover he had left out a word. When they came home, he seemed untroubled by the error and said he would sit up all night if necessary to re-do the whole page – and he did.

There is something extraordinary about mature men. They see the world so differently from women of similar age and that holds true even if we are all poets. Ken, Ian and Bill are all very good poets. They see things with a clarity that I find so refreshing and humbling because my own is usually subjective in some way, which is a quality many women poets share. Working with Stephen as our publisher enables me to have a privileged view of so many different types of poetry. I wonder where my writing will go in the future.

It seems to me that, all their lives, men have to be aware of the world around them as they follow their dreams/careers, and take on the responsibilities of partners and children. When they are older and the demands of life are less immediate, they can have more time for introspection and philosophy. I am certain this is reflected in their writing. Women, I believe, have to wait till we are older before we get the affirmation of our efforts. For most, it is when our children grow up and have children of their own. The affirmation adds to our strength and confidence and this is where we write from.

We have had a wonderful journey, but I am looking forward to going home. I long for silence and solitude to settle myself down. I am getting more at ease with the knowledge Ken has gone and there will be no more lunches with him, but he has given me something else – added confidence in myself – so it will be all right eventually. The funeral is on Friday morning. I am afraid of the pain this occasion, the surroundings, will evoke.

Bill and Kay arrived home after their long drive from the campus and we took them out to dinner as promised. A stately old pub, and the meals and surroundings were good. Kay asked us while we were eating who we thought we took after most, our mothers or fathers. There were interesting responses, especially from Stephen. It is something I need to think about a bit more because I don't know. Certainly something has come down through the Eldridge gene pool that makes me a dreamer and a doer.

Bairnsdale–Stawell

We chatted quietly with Bill over breakfast, but we had a long drive ahead again and it was time to start. I was intrigued how we would drive through the middle of Melbourne on a toll road.

It was a long road to Melbourne, with many areas disrupted by roadworks. In fact, extensive roadworks continued on and off almost to Stawell. We did pull in somewhere for coffee and I bought sandwiches for lunch later. I kept myself amused by keeping track (!) of the railway line that connects Bairnsdale and Melbourne. Perhaps I was tired, wary of what we were coming home to, but my enthusiasm seemed to drain as even the countryside became less interesting.

We passed Morwell. Not in itself particularly noteworthy except there had been a fire burning in the coal mine for weeks and residents had been evacuated, though possibly they had returned to their homes by now. Bill was right: we could, very briefly, see inside the big crater of the mine. There was evidence of fire over a big area. Burned and scorched bushes and trees lined the highway for what seemed like miles.

The traffic became heavier the closer we came to Melbourne. We drove through a long tunnel and then over the West Gate bridge. I have seen this bridge several times when transferring from the airport into Melbourne city centre but driving over it was truly awesome. Such an enormous structure and so very long. I suppose I had thought it was just to go over the river; I had no idea it was actually the bypass. It was challenging for Stephen to get in the right lane so we could head towards Ballarat.

Later, we passed Kryal Castle. I was suddenly shoved down memory lane again.

It was 1978. We had driven from Adelaide to Mount Gambier, along the Great Ocean Road to Warrnambool then up through Colac to Ballarat and then home to Adelaide. Twelve hundred miles in a week with a car with a damaged radiator, three boys under ten, and I was five months pregnant with the next child. Kryal Castle was in its infancy then. We stayed at the Welcome Stranger caravan park and took the boys to Sovereign Hill. We went in the underground mine and they also fossicked for gold. I never knew if the few grains they found had been planted there or not. I still have Mark's in a small bottle. Lovely images remain of them crouched in the creek with their sieves. How extraordinary that Stephen took Chris there only a couple of years later when they first came to Australia. Chris found some gold too which Stephen wrapped up in a tissue. Some while later, he tossed the tissue away, thinking it was rubbish. Oops.

We decided not to go into Ballarat but somewhere pulled in at one of the truck rest stops to have our sandwiches. I was aware again of the vastness of Australia. This had struck me when we took the Overland train to and from Melbourne last year and it was the Overland line that kept us company all the way back to Adelaide now. I was so pleased to see the Grampians again. We had seen them in the distance from the train and I was reminded of going there years earlier and rather wished we could get closer to them.

We drove into Stawell at about five p.m. and wandered along the high street. Some lovely buildings there but really we were tired and wanted to settle. There had been a large population of Chinese in the area who came in for the mining work. These days, the town only comes to life once a year for the Stawell Gift, a foot race in which people come from far and wide to participate. The names of some of the winners are carved in pavers down the high street.

We located a place for takeaway Asian food for dinner and set off to find our last motel of the journey. It was on the main highway, which proved interesting during the night when the heavy long-distance trucks trundled by. I even heard the lonesome and haunting wail of a freight train.

There are other lovely memories that have drifted from the past. For the first ten years in Australia, we lived in Salisbury next door to Greg and Elsie and their two daughters. Greg had been called up to do National Service and names like Sale, Wagga Wagga and Puckapunyal were places that Elsie spoke of, though they didn't mean anything to me. This trip, we have passed through Wagga Wagga and Sale and so Elsie's voice has been a presence.

As we drove up through Ararat, I was reminded that they came to live at a place called Snake Gully or Snake something in this area. It must have been in the mid-80s when they bought a log cabin and some land and came down to stay as often as possible before finally moving here. They brought me with them one weekend. I remember very green fields, very cold crisp air, a wonderful silence and the endless drive home towards the lowering evening sun. Things in my life were in a bad way then and I wish I could remember more.

It has been good to be reminded of people who have shown me kindness, and they certainly did.

Stawell–Adelaide

Was it me or the spirits of this land that made sleep elusive? I'm not certain. The past is being stirred and I want to reconcile it to its rightful place.

Driving back towards South Australia, I have been aware how the topography is changing. The Hay plains were flat and pale green. Since we left Melbourne behind, we have been driving through endless stretches of dried grass. Not the grey of dead grasses and dreary dried-up bushes that I didn't like on our way to Barmera and then on out to Mildura. The grasses in south-west Victoria are more golden, it's true, and perhaps by moonlight or when the wind blows, they have a silver sheen, but they also left me feeling like the earth, parched and gasping for breath and water. We were escorted all the time by either mountains in the distance or hills close by.

Well, they say the best-laid plans of mice and men… We were fortunate at this last motel that a cooked breakfast was included in the price. But we had woken to light drizzle and we could barely see the Grampians. Stephen had planned to take us off the main highway so we could drive close to them, but it just wasn't worth it with the rain. I was disappointed but it was probably for the best.

There have been several reminders of our vulnerability to fire here in Australia. Similar to Morwell, we drove for miles with burned and scorched bushes either side of us but, miraculously, so much new growth was appearing. This is a stunning country.

Our next déjà vu moment came near Nhill. In his book, Ian has a poem or two about the Australian poet John Shaw Neilson. As we motored along, we spotted a sign alerting us to a monument to an Australian poet ahead. Well, we had to stop and, yes, it was there in memory of John Shaw Neilson. I took photos to send to Ian later. Sometimes the world seems very small.

We had been travelling on the Western Highway but it changes its name to Dukes Highway at Bordertown. It is where Bob Hawke hails from. We drove around the town and then stopped for one last coffee and cake. The bakery was a large log cabin sort of place with lots of antiques about. It did have a lovely atmosphere. There was a gift shop attached – of course – and I found the right bear for Bertie, except it isn't a bear, it is an Eeyore the donkey from the Winnie the Pooh books but deliciously soft.

We availed of the public loos, which quixotically were in converted gaol cells. Then, as is often the way, there was one last thing to delight us. All those miles and miles of train tracks we had seen or crossed over since leaving Adelaide and no sighting of a single train. Then we heard a mournful howl and were rewarded by a freight train going over the level crossing. Stephen counted seventy-four wagons. It seemed to take ages for it to pass. It was a special moment.

South Australia is a harsh place geographically. It is only when you draw closer to the Murray river that it gentles.

We had a pause at Tailem Bend for petrol and time to look at the river. It holds a particular kind of magic for me here, but I'm not sure why. Perhaps it is simply that there are areas of green where water is pumped up to irrigate the earth.

We hurried past Murray Bridge, another place with memories of our Overland journey.

It seemed Mount Barker put on a special show for us. It was early afternoon and everything looked slightly hazy but we could see the shape so clearly against a pale sky.

Then of course it was back to very familiar territory, Crafers and Mount Lofty. The very practical freeway and the Heysen tunnel now deny travellers the magnificent sweeping views of the Adelaide plains, the city itself and Gulf St Vincent beyond as you come down out of the hills, but I remember them well, each bend gifting a sight to take my breath away. I can recall the sea shining like bronze in the late afternoon light of summer and skies painted pink as if by a giant artist's brush.

Back in Port Adelaide we collected the mail and picked up some bits and pieces from the supermarket and then it was home. The sun was shining; it felt like autumn. A check of the garden revealed that the plants had done very well without us, thank you very much. I put clean water in the bird baths and slowly unpacked our things.

What an extraordinary journey. A big circle that looks so small on the map of Australia. It is like the discoveries of the Northern Territory. It will take time to digest, and no doubt different things will remind me of where we went and who we met and the past will settle where it belongs, the depth that makes the present so glorious.

www.ingramcontent.com/pod-product-compliance
Lightning Source LLC
Chambersburg PA
CBHW030906080526
44589CB00010B/175